Daily Mantras From Maui

Daily Mantras From Maui

River Marilou Penner

Copyright © 2021 by River Marilou Penner.

ISBN:	Softcover	978-1-6641-5165-9
	eBook	978-1-6641-5164-2

All rights reserved. No part of this book may be reproduced or transmitted in any form or by any means, electronic or mechanical, including photocopying, recording, or by any information storage and retrieval system, without permission in writing from the copyright owner.

Any people depicted in stock imagery provided by Getty Images are models, and such images are being used for illustrative purposes only.
Certain stock imagery © Getty Images.

Print information available on the last page.

Rev. date: 01/14/2021

To order additional copies of this book, contact:
Xlibris
844-714-8691
www.Xlibris.com
Orders@Xlibris.com
822764

Daily Mantra

Introduction

What I have written in this book of mantras, I received somewhere along my life's journey; we stand on the shoulders of giants. What we have heard and regurgitate is plagiarism; what we have learned and integrated is shared wisdom. Nothing is uniquely mine. Before I could read, there was a barrier between author's experiences and insights and my ability to access and relate to it. When I crossed that barrier and learned to read, author's world became one with mine. In this book, I share with you the gems of my direct experiences, shaped by the wisdom of all who have influenced me. Among these influences are my clients. Mahalo for your trust, your wisdom and your open expression to growth. Mahalo also for sharing your magnificent journey, every one of you has touched my life in deep and meaningful ways.

I have also been guided by teachers such as Louise Haye, Mooji, Ram Das, Katherine Woodward Thomas, Richard Rohr and countless gift carriers of new thought and spirituality. Where I can reference the exact contribution, I will provide quotations and source references. Otherwise, I humbly acknowledge the presence of these teachers in my discoveries from intimate and direct experience in my soul.

My choices have been shaped and guided by my council of women. I have decided not to mention names here, we are an intimate circle of kind, loving, intelligent and wise females who have not gone unscathed by life. Women who have refused to crumble under the weight of sorrow, disappointment and loss. Women who hold each other up and provide listening, suggestions and perspective which I trust.

I have been given a leg up out of the illusion of fantasy through the painful and joyful union and ending of my intimate relationships as

I reflect on my part in the dance we shared of agreements and soul contracts from pure love.

The intention of these mantras from Maui are to serve and support your discoveries of channels to freedom from fear, anxiety, depression and patterns of unhealthy behaviors. As you use these mantras as your daily food for thought; ask, is what I read here going to assist? If not, give it no attention. Stay in the witnessing presence of your own experience; in the silent perceiving heart space. Don't give it to the mind; no need to suppress or control the mind, rather, stay in the heart and behold the beauty of God.

Love has come into focus for today's mantra. True friendship crosses all boundaries of race, species, gender, socio economic, status and world view. Love is our inherent natural state in which, from which our true selves' dwell. To fall in love and make one person a priority is practice love. To love is to know yourself. Fear creeps in from the conditioned mind; doubt of commitment, change of mind, suspicion, dislike changes the "thought" of love. Love is non changing. Love is touching, seeing, hearing, feeling, smelling everything expansively. It has been said there is either love or fear. Today, be in love by present awareness beyond mind's value system.

We live our greatest potential when we give up the fight. Peaceful beings stand on the foundation of choosing to let the grievances go. I believe that people act unconsciously when wounds of their past are unresolved. Talk therapy, therefore, is a sacred conversation where hurts are heard, and counsel is offered. New insights and ways of seeing and thinking resource us in participating in ways that create peace. There are many indigenous traditions that support this method of healing. Talking circles with elders where a structured process holds individuals accountable and restores connection. These mantras are invitations to seek ways of restoring connection with your true self and with others. My deepest intention is to inspire connection. Life is relational.

Mantra for Today

January 1, 2021

The first day of the rest of your life! It seems easy to truly understand the meaning of the words, "The past is over" today, especially as we begin a new decade. Let these words in deeply, "past is past". Whether this year will be a happy one depends on us! Make inner peace and compassion the main path today and each day and see for yourself if this doesn't bring happiness. Each of us is a contributor to happiness in our circles, each one a contributor to the care of our planet. It begins with inner peace and compassion. When the inner landscape is carefully attended to the extending space reflects this. Mindful choices based on conscious commitment to be an interior peace keeper.

Lovingly,
River

Mantra for Today

January 2, 2021

The year 2020 has given us 20/20 hindsight illuminating what doesn't work for the planet. We are now in a time of reflection and an opportunity to apply what we learn to a new and better normal. What seems evident is, it is time to give the feminine a turn at leadership. Equality, respect, self-determination and rights to all people is only sensible, and collaboration verses division needs to be our approach to conflict. Listening for understanding with one another verses "I know already". We need to take a humble approach to mistakes where "correct and continue" replaces exile and damnation. We are on the cusp of transition, isn't it obvious that our world is giving us every sign? Today, practice letting go of worn out ideas and long held beliefs and position yourself in an open space, mentally and spiritually and be open to participate in co-creating something better for all life on earth; something sustainable for now and the future.

Lovingly,
River

Mantra for Today

January 3, 2021

Everything is for our growth. Emotional affairs can feel devastating in a couple. Once the initial shock subsides there is a rich opportunity to face the truth. Emotional affairs are the gateway to a vista of factors causing disconnection in the primary relationship. The heart longs to be known. When a couple fall into the mundane, a certain taking for granted happens. Not having the communication skills to bid to have needs met makes ripe the potential for a stranger to sing the hearts song. See it not as betrayal but rather take ownership for where each partner has betrayed their own needs for intimacy by being silent when conversation would be helpful. Many couples are shell shocked by conversation becoming hostile, so, they avoid conflict by suppressing their feelings. This makes an emotional affair easy to consider. Happiness comes when we do not hold our partner responsible for our inner comfort; taking responsibility for how we contribute to intimacy is key. Open honest non-blaming and non- accusing communication is a skillful way to keep the bond exclusive. Everything is an opportunity to grow. Today I use the hurt to look at myself, I am willing to change.

Lovingly,
River

Mantra for Today

January 4, 2021

True empowerment is owning your experience. Self-accountability is more than responsibility, it is committing to personal growth through the emotional reactions stimulated by relationships. Whenever we blame the other, we give away our dignity, we reduce ourselves to victims. Moving through life in this way is to be stuck in childhood. Inner work is healing work. On this trajectory, we make ourselves available to relationships. We come to the relationship whole, willing to collaborate. No greater hell is there than living at the mercy of trigger reactions. Put down your defenses and go within. Here you will find your pure precious self-waiting for your compassion and release from the personal prison of illusionary victimization. Today, notice all the ways the finger is pointed at other and turn it towards self; not to blame self but to lovingly take the reins and heal the barriers to clear understanding.

Lovingly,
River

Mantra for Today

January 5, 2021

Where have we learned that punishment and harsh approaches bring favorable results? Childhood is rot with abuse at the hands of primary care givers. Children are verbally reprimanded, restrained and physically disciplined and yet behaviors are not corrected, they go covert at best. Why are we not raised with loving lessons of understanding and guidance? To persuade cooperation and train with lessons and natural consequences through means such as fables and loving compassion, would raise healthy minds and free spirits. Too many adults today are reactive beings, dysfunctional and rebellious. Today, reparenting self through ceremony of reclaiming childhood, committing to nonviolence towards self or other. Experiment today with seeing results from kind approaches verses the automatic reaction of punitive intentions.

Lovingly,
River

Mantra for Today

January 6, 2021

Not everything that is faced can be changed; but nothing can be changed until it is faced. —James Baldwin (1924–1987)

Conflict is part of every relationship. To be human is to error. When friction between people is not skillfully addressed, resentments build. With resentment comes stories or versions of perceived reality around the conflict. In couples work, the best skill is to listen for understanding, paraphrase what was heard, validate, giving the gift of non-judgment, and empathize, the gift of feeling intimately into the other person. The greatest insult to injury in relationship conflict is avoidance, passive aggressively making oneself unavailable to hold sacred space for clearing the hurt and suffering brought by conflict. In my experience, people repeat their grievances for years until they feel truly heard. Today, skillful listening.

Lovingly,
River

Mantra for Today

January 7, 2021

Every one of us is shadowed by an illusory person: a false self. This is the man I want myself to be but who cannot exist, because God does not know anything about him. And to be unknown of God is altogether too much privacy. —Thomas Merton

In our lives of personality, socially seen and assigned roles, we lose contact with our true nature. There is a time to retract and a time to expand. We know when to do which based on the energy felt. Mindfulness is a current practice in the modern world to presence oneself in felt energy. Access to truth through contemplation makes clear who I am vs who desire wants me to be. Today contact with spirit through stillness.

Lovingly,
River

Mantra for Today

January 8, 2021

To believe that we are separate and must remain known for who we portray ourselves as, is to fall into the deepest pit of endless effort. Attachment to the false self is attachment to youth, health, beauty, status, story, external validation. Effort is endless to maintain the image of the false self. True self is one with all life. True self is love, creativity, vibrational frequency, expansive presence. No effort is required to be who you are. Let the body age. Let the cycles of human life phase on, you remain. How do I detach from the false self? No longer attending to the mind's nudging's. Stop thought. Connect to that observing presence of being, there is no judgment, no fear, no negativity.

Lovingly,
River

Mantra for Today

January 9, 2021

There are two selves living in one life. The false self, who brings judgment, comparisons, defensiveness, and a strong need to be right, and the true Self, who is the unseparated source of love. We easily confuse who we are as the false self. We get fearful that we must fight for our rights, that we are not good enough, that we are not worthy. From here we act in anger. True self, our true nature knows our worth is immeasurable, there is no need for defense, there is a complete acceptance to the unfolding of what is. If change is needed, from a place of true self, we make changes where we can with sanity. True self, in worldly terms, is sane. Most humans are reactive and imagining threats to their false self-image. Stop the insanity. Turn towards who you truly are.

Lovingly,
River

Mantra for Today

January 10, 2021

As a woman in her fall season, there is a certain broader view. Shedding ideas and ideals of what life should look like, there is the beauty of surprise beyond imagination. The joy of seeing a child fall in love with a chicken, and the love reciprocated! Meeting strangers that feel instantly like family. Reinventing previously contracted relationships reflecting greater truths than before. Earlier seasons were devoted to my story, fantasized versions of myself, now, all that matters are being one with all life, undefined, without title or label or status or place. As with all life, I inherently belong with all. Today, presence.

Lovingly,
River

Mantra for Today

January 11, 2021

Creating new agreements. Love is an experience of fullness and emptiness. We are hollowed out from the person we once were to the person we are becoming based on the great lessons and influential experiences that the relationship brought. When a relationship ends we naturally feel scorned, as the saying goes, hell hath no fury... once the anger has served its purpose, to generate the type of energy required to move forward, it's best to lay down the sword and accept life on life's terms. Rumi said, it seems like the end, it looks like a sunset but in reality it is the dawn. Wonder of wonders, it may be possible that your greatest potential is after the fall of your current idea of yourself. Everything in life is like a birthing process; we feel agony, we say no! We try to pretend this is not happening, we say, not now, not this, but the birth is in process. The best thing to do, the only thing, is to find the courage and commit to the birth and remember the gift at the end of this pain is precious new life.

Lovingly,
River

Mantra for Today

January 12, 2021

There is a certain cycle all living being energetically move through. We strive for a fixed sense of certainty, yet nothing in the natural world is fixed or stable. We naturally go through a deconstruction or disorder from known to unknown. This is happening now, in this global pandemic. You may be experiencing disorder, change and uncertainty in your personal life as well. Everywhere there is disorder and uncertainty. Trust dear one, that what follows is a new order, a reconstruction, like a rebirthing of something more aligned with a higher purpose. Even though there may be a feeling of confusion and anxiety, as we breathe through the contractions, eventually it softens and there is ease again.

Lovingly,
River

Mantra for Today

January 13, 2021

This or something better. As keen observers of change, we notice that life is a constant flow of shifts and changes. Technological changes in the past 50 years, a relatively short time frame, have taken us "from a rotary phone to a touch-tone or keypad phone, or even from a landline to a wireless phone, a disruptive technology displaces established assumptions, as in, say, combining a phone, a camera, a computer, a music library and player, a GPS device, and a mobile Internet portal." (Richard Rohr from the Center of Action and Contemplation.) We adapt to new situations after a brief resistance phase and eventually it becomes the new norm. The gift of change (hopefully)is growth and an expansion to greater expressions of love, acceptance and connection to truth. It is not easy to let go of long held attachments to identity and ego status. Once we wake up to see, the only threat is fear, a (fantasized experience appearing real), we can relax and trust in our abilities to flex and adapt. Motto for today, This or something better. Trusting in the source of all good we turn our challenges into our championship.

Lovingly,
River

Mantra for Today

January 14, 2021

When we were impressionable young children, we created meaning about ourselves and our roles in the world based on the environments we were raised in. For many of us childhood set the course of our interactions with others in a "survival" like dynamic. To not need or to be useful in order to be loved, for example, sets the stage for over functioning in a relationship and acquiescing to the sole needs of others. When we become aware of our unconscious source fracture story, (a term coined by Katherine Woodward Thomas), we can begin to relate with people in a more mutually fulfilling way, honoring ourselves and also the other. We are here to wake up, dear one, to unconscious patterns that at one time did serve to keep us alive but now we must shift out of those old worn out patterns and thrive!

Lovingly,
River

Mantra for Today

January 15, 2021

When we say, I have to work on myself, we are saying, I am liberating myself from the prison of my mind. I am freeing myself from false beliefs of not worthy or not good enough. When we "work on ourselves", we are declaring that now I am ready to break old patterns of thinking and behaving. When we go to therapy, we are sitting in the temple of our own highest potential. Letting go of old ways of relating to ourselves and others and expanding into truth. You are a divine being, one with all other beings, when we relate with this understanding, there is compassion for those who hurt us and forgiveness for believing we didn't deserve any better.

Lovingly,
River

Mantra for Today

January 16, 2021

As we season in life, it is time to move out of identity claiming and survival mindset to shedding the ego self and thriving. Few humans reach full adulthood; clinging to stories of "who I was", rather than harvesting the gem of wisdom and letting go of the image of greatness. In the first phase of life, we need to establish ourselves as somebodies, programmed to get attention and be validated as worthy of a place on stage; thereby belonging. If in later life we still strive to declare, this is who I am, I am me, see me", we reveal a wounded part that is lost, still seeking place. To admit and attend to our wounds with humility and vulnerability we wake up to knowing ourselves from a witness standpoint. From here we can look with eyes unblinking and lovingly move ourselves into maturity, beyond surviving into thriving.

Lovingly,
River

Mantra for Today

January 17, 2021

It is important to watch how we story who we are. If we tell ourselves and others that who we are is reflected on our losses, we invite more of the same. If a relationship has ended, we may say, I was a bad judge of character. This brings in doubt when new love walks towards you. A certain skepticism floods the pure space of possibility. Once you get through the hurt and anger that loss has left, you start to remember the beautiful aspects, and if you are committed to growth, you see the hard times as gifts. Growth is our trajectory. Do not be scarred by deceit, betrayal and disappointment. If you cannot let go, let be. Everything is a lesson. When the hurt resurfaces, Just notice without story, this is a natural experience, memories can leave us unstable. Smile upon yourself dear one, you have loved without filters, everyone you have invited in has been an angel. Love with beginners' heart, knowing that based on all the previous experiences, you are now more resourced to choose wisely.

Lovingly,
River

Mantra for Today

January 18, 2021

It is often in the darkness of despair and loss that we find our light. We are students of this life. We have these amazing barometers, our bodies, that carry the heavy heart of grief, or the bubbly joy of hope, or the tightness of pending harm. As we learn to trust our bodies we take guidance from a physical knowing. Every loss, every disappointment, every being who has crossed our path is a teacher who holds the lantern lighting the path to truth. It is truth that sets us free. Where are you holding doubt? Give that part some compassion and understanding and see if it can loosen a little. If the shadow can be perceived as having no authentic existence in itself but are mere reactions and defenses, we can give space and distance with a sense of courage to move through difficult experiences. My loving support is with you dear one,

Lovingly,
River

Mantra for Today

January 19, 2021

When we stop resisting reality and put all the cards face up on the table, real freedom comes. There are myriad ways of relating. Traditional marriage can be stifling, each individual is constantly evolving and expanding to be who they were born to be. When I come from a deeper, steadier, and quieter place in my heart and mind, I celebrate the unfolding and dance joyfully for myself and my beloved. Today I let it all wash to shore and get my feet wet and dance. There are no catastrophes only possibilities.

Lovingly,
River

Mantra for Today

January 20, 2021

We don't know until we know. Innocently or ignorantly we engage and commit with high ideals when the heart urns for belonging. Few of us have experienced true belonging as children. We childlike ones reach for companionship, for home for identity, we need to be cherished so that we can know ourselves. The denied emotions of childhood lay suppressed, we haven't learned how to express, the cost, authenticity. No relationship can survive inauthenticity. So, the search begins again. Like the book, Chicken Little, we ask, "Are you my mother?", to any animated object. Inner work is remembering who you are. Once you find yourself, any place is home.

Lovingly,
River

Mantra for Today

January 21, 2021

Marion Woodman wrote, "Children not loved for who they are do not learn how to love themselves. Their growth is an exercise in pleasing others, not in expanding through experience."

Real love requires us to expose our wounded parts and surrender our defenses. If we haven't learned to love ourselves we avoid true intimacy and become addicted to work or other distractions that gain us approval but keep our true selves behind closed doors. To break free of these patterns of behavior in relationship to one self and others, we must learn to inquire within. Getting InTouch with feelings and emotions and beliefs and becoming honest with what is alive in us. Pause for a moment dear one and speak or write what your direct experience is in this moment. See what wants your attention. See what you are resisting. It is never too late to retrieve the lost child within and bring up to date the wounded parts. In loving ourselves for who we are, our intelligence, sexuality, characteristics, personal preferences, needs and wants, we begin to stand on solid ground. As we become honest with ourselves we live authentically.

Lovingly,
River

Mantra for Today

January 22, 2021

When you were a baby, beyond the need for nourishment and shelter, you had a fundamental need to be gazed at by a loving mother. Her eyes seeing you, attuned to your magnificence you would have a sense of who you are through the mirrors of her eyes. If this was not your experience, you likely dwell with shame running in the dark recesses of your psyche. Psychologist, Carl Jung described shame as "a soul-eating emotion. Shame, like a master, leaves us slave to a state of "obligation to our wounding mothers--to keep pleasing or achieving, remain stoic, unconscious, or angry. We can't imagine what life would be like without shame because in a twisted sense it has been a kind of caretaker to us. Shame leads us to the defenses that we mistakenly believe will protect or comfort us. It becomes part of our self-concept.

It's important to add here that these defenses probably have protected us or comforted us along the way. As children, we needed to disappear into our imaginations or become stoic in order to learn to meet our own needs, in order to cope and survive." (Daily Om; The Mother Wound). The healing begins when we retrieve our wounded child and become that caring loving mother. If you are able to receive this loving gaze from a trusted friend or therapist practice compassionately letting your child part feel this deep reverence of your divinity dear one. Remember you are a spiritual being having a human experience, it is your homework to heal.

Lovingly,
River

Mantra for Today

January 23, 2021

If we don't change, we don't grow. If we don't grow, we aren't really living. -Gail Sheehy

It is often said that change is the only constant in life. Yet us humans are evolutionarily predisposed to resist change because of the risk associated with it - the possible gains or losses. Despite this resistance to change, it is more important than ever. In current society the pace of change is faster, and it will only continue to accelerate. It seems that the only option is to hop on the train, or get left behind, stuck, inauthentic, unhappy. The ones that don't embrace change are bound to lose ground and stagnate. While you are anxiously anticipating change or in the midst of a challenging one, remember my love, you are amazingly beautiful just the way you are! Today hold your head high, and keep plowing through, there's a pot of gold at the end of each and every rainbow.

Lovingly,
River

Mantra for Today

January 24, 2021

Forgiveness is the necessary practice towards true freedom. When we hold resentments from the past, we carry a certain burden deep within. Forgiveness doesn't mean we no longer hold the other person accountable for their actions, nor do we condone their behavior. Instead, forgiveness is cutting the cord of vibrations between the two of you. It doesn't mean you now go to full trust; no, we learn to use decrement. Forgiveness is a spiritual practice; seeing the other person's actions as their wounded self. There is a divine pure and loving being within the wounded reactive part. Forgiveness is knowing that part exists while at the same time giving yourself some space from the part in that person which harmed you. Forgiveness takes time, begin the process by feeling the emotions within you, understand where the hurtful acts stem from and lovingly commit to self-care. All this applies to self-forgiveness as well, precious.

Lovingly,
River

Mantra for Today

January 25, 2021

Learning to communicate directly creates closeness and prevents misunderstandings, hurt feelings and resentments. When we believe our feelings are wrong, we may adopt a stoic stance to prevent exposing those feelings. There are no wrong emotions, emotions are energy in motion, they wave in and out; so long as we do no harm. Sometimes feelings point to something that needs our attention. Better to examine feelings than to suppress them. Many of us engage in passive aggressive behavior. This means suppressing our true feelings and portraying what we think is a less confrontational stance. In the world of psychology, this is a disordered way of being. It is inauthentic and leads to confusion, dissatisfaction and ultimately disconnection in relationships. Many of us are conflict phonics, ironically however, by pretending to be fine when we are uncomfortable leads to conflict which eats away the relationship like rust. Beginning today, be truthful and clear in communication and reap the rewards of authenticity. All cards face up on the table.

Lovingly,
River

Mantra for Today

January 26, 2021

Being seen and acknowledged for something we've done instead of for who we are creates an identity of worth through productivity. The accolades and admiration for the outcome of our creativity or service lands lightly because we've become conditioned to see ourselves as valuable only when we do something. It is important to embrace those friends and loved ones who are eagerly showing us our value is in our simple presence, in the miracle of our existence ; and all the doing is bonus but not necessarily in order to be loved. Brainwashed into thinking our success in "doing" defines us, aging folk become depressed, feel worthless and a burden when the doing part expires. Aging gracefully means loving yourself and opening your heart to loving others. Walk in love dear one, love is right there in you as your natural attraction.

Lovingly,
River

Mantra for Today

January 27, 2021

When we are children, we learn that in order to have freedom we must behave. This programming sets the stage for a life time of belief that our value is dependent on the positive regard of others. The word persona refers to the mask or facade that shields or hides aspects we have learned are not cherished by people close to us. A spiritual practice gets us in touch with our true nature, our authenticity, freeing us to discover our true identity and our own heart's desire. Uncovering our truth, we clear the blocks that keep us shut down and isolated in our dark private minds. This is where deviance seeps out to release the pressure of being good in order to be loved. Still your mind dear one and tune into the genuine reality of your divine being, and from there move into living life, unapologetically you.

Lovingly,
River

Mantra for Today

January 28, 2021

Richard Rohr, an influential spiritual teacher, expresses that we are not punished for our sins but rather we punish ourselves when we refuse to be accountable for the wrongs we do. Accountability is powerful in repairing and reconnecting with our higher selves and with others. He states, "...the punishment I'm inflicting on myself when I remain unconscious of the fears and judgments that drive my behavior. When I am not in honest relationship and present to my whole self, I am much further away from the Divine Presence who forgives everything." We cannot experience true forgiveness from self or other when we turn a blind eye to our hurtful actions. Today sweet one, have the self-love and courage to take an honest inventory of the harm you have done to yourself and others. The response may surprise and transform your relationship with yourself and other.

Lovingly,
River

Mantra for Today

January 29, 2021

We human beings are complex to say the least. I choose to believe that at the core we are all divine and that a possibility exists in us all to be equanimous, loving and fair. When we are out of balance however, and out of touch with our true selves, we can become paranoid defended and vengeful. No one is exempt from dualism. It has been my experience that my life fairs better when I respond from a balanced healthy state. When hurt and fear lead, destruction touches not only the object of attack but every aspect of one's own life as well. Find your center dear one. Return to your spirit self and choose to navigate from love and fairness. My loving support is with you always.

Lovingly,
River

Mantra for Today

January 30, 2021

In the world we live in currently, we are faced with challenges that invite deepening our practice of mindfulness. The pandemic status of the Coronavirus could cause hysteria and nerve-wracking fear to replace clear thinking and thoughtful action. The world has faced epic threats before, examples of human reaction show various responses. Be calm in the face of this world wide epidemic and take action to walk in a good way. We now have the opportunity to be conscious in a new way. We may have eagerly greeted one another with a warm hug, now we stand apart and gaze into the other eyes and bow, "may you be well." We carelessly would have sneezed or handled door knobs, now we mindfully cover our nose and mouth honoring all those around us and mindfully in the moment wipe the handle before we turn it. We may have thought nothing of going into public places, now we may choose to remain home and be present with ourselves and our loved ones. It all becomes meditation. Stress and fear lower the immune system, we have the choice now to affirm our bodies with gratitude, thanking our immune system for working so beautifully to fight disease. The serenity prayer, "Grant me the serenity to accept the things I cannot change, the courage to change the things I can, and the wisdom to know the difference." Applies now. Be calm dear one and mindful. Take suggestions to protect yourself and others and use this time to practice mindfulness.

Lovingly,
River

Mantra for Today

January 31, 2021

Everything is unfolding exactly as it should. We humans are one of the natural worlds. Like butterflies and dinosaurs, we too are affected by climate, pressures, food choices and airborne viruses. Fear not the future, for you do not know what is to come. Fear is like asking to experience now what you don't want. Instead, be the best human you can be. Slow down and take inventory of your life. Are you having the conversations that inspire yourself and the listener? Are you softening the world for yourself and others through kindness? Now is the time to put aside grievances and held resentments and move more consciousness than ever before. What we have now is an opportunity to be great, wise and the highest potential for love. Everything is exactly as it should be, and we are blessed.

Lovingly,
River

Mantra for Today

February 2, 2021

There are times, like the one we are currently experiencing, where changes and uncertainty leave us in an unfamiliar place. We may not have chosen to be hurled into isolation and questionable economic futures, but here we are. If we allow the feelings and emotions stage for our observation they help us get in touch with a deeper sense that has been there for a long time. When we feel something intensely we may have an urge to push it down or numb it out. It may keep us up at night and leave us less resourced to function. This could be the dark nights of the soul. Use it for all it's worth, dear one. Follow the threat and see if you can discover what is ripe for transformation in you. Is there a belief that you don't belong? And all the performing and posturing hasn't resulted in that true embrace? Is there a grasping and clawing behavior to find your rightful place in the family of life? Having used mind altering options, physical sensations and avoiding mental, emotional and relational challenges, it all leaves you with the same gaping hole. Stillness is your bridge now to a place of self-recognition, the I who observes the life, that one is you, the rest is personality. You are home right here, at peace in your true nature beyond personality. Here life happens where there is acceptance. You got this!

Lovingly,
River

Mantra for Today

February 3, 2021

Today's mantra is inspired by Richard Rohr's Center for Action and Contemplation. Forgetting who we are is an indescribable burden weighing 500 pounds, bleeding our will to live from our life force. The first script (our false self) has influenced the personal experience of expectations, attachments, demands and worry. These illusionary disappointments cause suffering and confusion, grasping and clinging to identity and position, recognition and validation. The struggle is felt intensely flooding us with all kinds of hurt. Remembering your true nature lifts this heavy script and liberates the soul to shine in every life event. How do I get there? you ask. It is the pain and joy that brings us to our edge (or our knees), and we simply let go of the back-breaking beliefs about ourselves and others. We find our self at the still place where there are no roles, no effort, no identity to project. Here we move towards our sage wise self that knows, everything is temporary, except real love.

Lovingly,
River

Mantra for Today

February 4, 2021

When people come together with a common cause or commitment, all differences and personal agendas disappear, and we are united. Reflecting on historical examples of this on a large scale; the civil rights movement, the equal rights movement, and many conscious commitments to make our world a fairer and kinder place for all of us to live, we see the beauty of humanity. Currently we are in a worldwide pandemic crisis, calling us all to be aware of our behavior. This is good for us! It is like mindfulness is the new religion. Mindfulness can only bring more awareness of the effects of our actions. It is easy to revert to old patterns of behavior, dear one, we all tend to want what we want and want it now. See this time as an opportunity to break the unconscious drive for instant gratification and continue to be part of the community effort to heal. This healing will affect each one of us personally and spiritually as well as keep our neighbors safe. Remain with the program to end the spread of the corona virus by thinking of others before yourself when making choices.

This is our spiritual practice now.

Lovingly,
River

Mantra for Today

February 5, 2021

As a trauma therapist I have come to know that the early childhood attachment experience sets the stage for future relationships. The insecure feeling of not being cherished by a primary caregiver, leaves a person forever longing to be loved and seen. Our hearts yearn for someone we can trust absolutely— when betrayal of this occurs again and again the template of disappointment is placed even upon the evidence of love as present. As a species, we are in a collective trauma of lost love. In this time of fear as we are inundated by news feeds of doom, fear clouds access to clear seeing and intuitive wisdom and knowledge is inaccessible. Remember dear one, you are divine in an earthy dynamic. Divine love can never fail. It may seem naive to shift the focus from the pandemic protocols and practices to isolate and stay away from each other, and yet, this is starting to feel like a divide and conquer propaganda. As humans we need one another. Remain in contact with loved ones and tap into your inner wisdom. If our love is not at the foundation of action, we fall prey to fear mongering. Peace is within you, love is your set point, open yourself to being loved beginning with self-love and compassion for the trauma of hurt and loss.

Lovingly,
River

Mantra for Today

February 6, 2021

You have been walking on earth constantly touched by ideas of who you are. The roles you play, the family you were born into, these are not you. These are circumstances. When we get wrapped up in identifying ourselves and reactive to the things that upset us, we forget we are free. Choose to be happy, "even though and especially when", dear one. Be happy even in the disappointment, even in the uncertainty, remember who you are. How?, you ask. By paying attention to what makes you light up. What is it for you? Your animals? Your creative expression? Your service? Music? Poetry? Spiritual inspiration? Physical movement? Gardening? Certain people? Focusing on being one with your hearts joy, will reconnect you to your birth right to happiness. This life is a happily ever after life!

Lovingly,
River

Mantra for Today

February 7, 2021

As we globally continue to isolate ourselves from the inter mingling and busyness of life, we might consider, since spring is gilding along the edges of seasonal change, put our hands in the earth. You don't have to live on a farm to take a shoe box add soil and seeds and water and light and create your own garden. Being one with nature, is the most natural thing to all species. We are nature. The Covid pandemic, although devastating in some ways, is a blessing in disguise as well. To reduce the effects of depression, caused by a disconnection to our true source; it is truly therapeutic to participate in some way with nature. One of the most influential books I have read on trees was, Braiding Sweet Grass, by Ethnobotanist, author, and Potawatomi elder Robin Kimmerer. She asserts, "We need acts of restoration, not only for polluted waters and degraded lands, but also for our relationship to the world. We need to restore honor to the way we live, so that when we walk through the world we don't have to avert our eyes with shame, so that we can hold our heads high and receive the respectful acknowledgment of the rest of [the] earth's beings." Do yourself and the planet a favor, dear one, and grow something. If not grow, then sit still under a tree and consider the now ancestor who planted it, knowing they would not live to sit under its shade. Today's word: appreciation.

Lovingly,
River

Mantra for Today

February 8, 2021

To be compassionate and tenderhearted towards those who hurt us is less likely if we cannot first generously practice these qualities to ourselves. There is rarely a human that has not experienced some sort of rejection, judgment or ill treatment in their lives. These experiences, if not addressed through compassion and tender care, can drive deep into the psyche leaving the person feeling flawed. You are not flawed, there is not something inherently wrong with you, dear one; you may have unattended wounds that still to this day leave a residual effect. Turn inwards with tenderness, feel where in the body these emotions reside and bring to those hurts understanding and love. We do not see people as they are, we see people as we are. Until we heal ourselves, we cannot truly see other. Feel my embrace.

Lovingly,
River

Mantra for Today

February 9, 2021

Each person and situation we encounter, offers us growth. If a person is critical and hurtful, if we feel rejected and hurt, we can learn how criticism harms. This learning, though painful, holds the potential to practice kindness to others. Let us not repeat the cruel treatments visited upon us but let us transform that behavior by doing better towards others. Martin Luther King preached, "Hate begets hate; violence begets violence; toughness begets a greater toughness. We must meet the forces of hate with the power of love". (1958) We do not have to be robotic mirrors of the hurt we have experienced. Not only do we change the world by doing the opposite, but we heal ourselves as well. When we can heal ourselves of the hurt we have experienced, we can truly show loving kindness to a world so in need of this.

Much love and compassion always,
River

Mantra for Today

February 10, 2021

Here, the year 2020, and still decades of movements publicly protesting against racism, sexism and hate have not brought us to a just society. People in the United States are waking up to the injustices of inequality, yet there remain hateful misguided people ravaging, looting and rioting. The president meets this situation with like-minded sentiment, "you loot, we shoot". We do not have to affirm this energy by becoming angry and reacting in harsh retaliation. Instead, (to be cliche), what the world needs is love. Love in action meets negativity with optimism, defending those marginalized by standing publicly showing solidarity against injustice, kindness to all people, nonviolence in speech and action, community gardening, service and especially voicing our support for a just world. We are what we think, with our thoughts and actions, we make the world. (Buddha).

Lovingly,
River

Mantra for Today

February 11, 2021

It begins with me. How we do anything, is how we do everything. Being with all of our human experience is different when we respond collectively towards change. Currently in our world injustices have fueled radical retaliation. Looting and rioting and violence are some people's best thinking to address the brutality and arrogant authority of a few. No life is insignificant, no injustice minor, we must avenge the loss of innocent people acted against because of the color of their skin. The pen is mightier than the sword. Communicating intolerance for police brutality through public protest, demanding stronger constraint protocol on the police would make far greater an impact than random terrorism in the communities in which we live. There are among us, those who will take advantage to express their anger that lurks beneath the surface illuminating their own personal unresolved traumas. Be the voice of change through peaceful means. Denounce violence and crime through the use of your values. Sign petitions, love your neighbors, forgive yourself and others. Defend the marginalized with wise speech. Change from the inside out. Make your mantra: "It begins with me".

Lovingly,
River

Mantra for Today

February 12, 2021

Life is one continuous flow of grace. Generosity flows from the abundance of love from all kinds of unexpected places. For me, yesterday Kale and tomatoes from one, plants freely shared, avocados from another, a baby goat placed in my trusting hands, support from friends, open hearted conversation, forgiveness for my mistakes, understanding. All grace! Living porous allows love in, presence allows recognition of all the good. Notice the continuous flow of grace dear one and relax in knowing, you are cherished.

Lovingly,
River

Mantra for Today

February 13, 2021

There are a few real gems, or keys of wisdom that make all the difference as we face change, uncertainty and that which we have no power to influence. Acceptance and Adaptability. We can only truly accept, once we first allow our feelings, thoughts and emotions expression. The trick is not to act on them but to at least release them. Without full exploration, repression masquerades as acceptance. Make no mistake, repression may appear like contentment, but woe is he who overlooks this distinction. Repression manifests as disfunction eventually. Adaptability comes following acceptance based on conscious expression of all facets of the situation until you find peace with it. If the situation involves a relationship dynamic which makes no space for expression, express through art, writing, or speaking to a trusted listener. What is your deepest desire? Under all the fear of uncertainty, under the disappointment, under the angst, what true wish for yourself lays there?

Lovingly,
River

Mantra for Today

February 14, 2021

Today is popularly known as Valentine's Day, a day of romance. Originally, in France and England February 14th was thought to be the day birds chose a mate. Today, a signified day for love can bring opportunity to make special effort to show love to one's beloved. Others face this day with heart ache. Love is our human base. Love is found in the helping an elder carry her bags, smiling at a tearful child with compassion, listening with an open heart, and forgiving ourselves and others. This day is for you dear one, spread your love widely and love will flow to you, from you and all around you.

Lovingly,
River

Mantra for Today

February 15, 2021

Throughout history inequality has caused suffering to women, people whose skin is not white, the uneducated, and the poor. There is a hierarchy visible and invisible setting the standards of whose voice is listened to and who is ignored. We are capable of correcting this injustice by first recognizing the subtle ways we discount those near us. The hurts unheard, the needs unmet drive a deep root of harm into the individual which ultimately affects the whole of humanity. Begin by making space available for conversation. Nonviolent listening means listening without being defensive, listening for the intent of what is being expressed, listening with compassion. When pain is first expressed it may not be eloquent or scripted in perfect prose, so listening without judgment is essential for healing. There is hope for a Just world, it begins with you and me dear friends.

Lovingly,
River

Mantra for Today

February 16, 2021

A personal narrative is a powerful script that places squarely before the mind's eye a lens through which the world is seen and believed. It is important to question the story we tell ourselves. Stories can be locked doors behind which we live, thinking we are safe. So common is it to hear a person describe their life in review, as hard. This story not only describes the life history, but also sets the stage for the next episode of "hard life". It is not exactly natural to question the mind but know that all descriptions are like little locks securing windows as well as doors around you. What would it be like to, with blanket statement, declare, "my life is growth, expansion, change, wonderful, a story of resilience"! Think if all the ways you label yourself and ask, is this freeing me or locking me up?

Lovingly,
River

Mantra for Today

February 17, 2021

When we move into an empty house, we soon fill it with furnishing, things, decorations and each and every nook and cranny become filled up. There is always something that tickles our fancy, this thing and that attracts our attention. The mind is like this. Thoughts of the past, interpretations, impressions, opinions, judgments, assessments begin to crowd the once open space of pure awareness. The way to bliss is non attachment to thoughts. The mind is like a butterfly in your face, demanding your attention. From a place of observation, it is just amusing, not distracting. Meditation is stillness, openness and spaciousness. As your breath in, expand your space, as your breath out empty your mind. Is your mind disturbing you? Remember, you are not your mind, not your thoughts. If sitting still is challenging, walk. Keep the focus on breathing in expansion, breathing out empty.

Lovingly,
River

Mantra for Today

February 18, 2021

Gandhi's famous quote, "Be the change you wish to see in the world", offers a profound and powerful suggestion that when actively practiced impacts us personally. We need to be loved, so love others. We need to be heard, so listen. We need to be acknowledged for our contribution, so give recognition. We need to be respected, so show respect. We want others to see our good intentions beyond our behavior, so assume the best in others. We don't want others to gossip about us, so do not gossip. As we shape our expressions of ourselves, we create the environment we need for our thriving. Life is a gift, as we give the best to the people around us, we dwell in the field we create.

Lovingly,
River

Mantra for Today

February 19, 2021

Loosen the grip. Recognize today what you cling to. Identity, skin color, physical appearance, sexual orientation, status, grievances, patterns, roles, beliefs, opinions, knowledge, all of it tightly gripped, all ideas of personal self. Who am I without these? Unbound. Let go of all these ideas for a time, is there peace? When it is recognized, the grip loosens and there is space. Liberation from personal identity allows true nature, presence. Each day we are born anew. Words are spells; when we carelessly spout thoughts based on reactions to perceived threats, we attract fear and negativity. Remember who you are, a powerful creator of your own movie. What you say, is so. It is not easy changing a habitual (knee jerk) reaction to the multiple stimulus in your life, but it is possible. Today, I choose to speak with emphasis on what is going well, on the gifts and contributions others generously bring to my life and forgive automatically the areas of disappointment. This moment by moment practice assures a life of peace and confidence that everything is happening for my growth.

Lovingly,
River

Mantra for Today

February 20, 2021

Everything is grace. We do not necessarily choose (consciously), to experience loss, heart ache, or suffering. Yet, troubled times offer the greatest profound insights and awakening. Consider the dissatisfaction is propelling you towards greater understanding. We want to be content, to experience pleasure without pain. Consider whatever crisis is here, is a gift needed for the greatest expansion. Allow suffering to shape you, to break you of your ignorance and suffuse you with joy. Joy and true love are one in the same.

Lovingly,
River

Mantra for Today

February 21, 2021

When we experience struggle there is an opportunity to adjust our goals, plans and behaviors. We learn in the struggle that something needs attention. Is it thought habits? Is it attitude? Are its old beliefs that behoove us? Is it relationship patterns in which we lose ourselves? These are the gifts of struggle. When we are comforted, we risk going back to sleep. We risk rocking back into our rut. So, use the struggle, milk it for all it's worth. The gems harvested serve to make us rich in important ways.

Lovingly,
River

Mantra for Today

February 22, 2021

If we think of ourselves and others in each other's lives to be of service to move towards our highest potential, everything that happens is helpful. Helping each other isn't always in the form we enjoy. At times a direct word, or a separation, or something even felt as hurtful, is a catalyst for our growth. Be in pure awareness of the people and circumstances that trigger you as powerful opportunities for important change. What needs to drop away? Is it a belief? A behavior? A habit? What is the action of another covertly offering as a blessing in disguise? If our actions or words cause another to suffer, ask was the intention rooted in love? Then let the other's reaction be theirs for their growth. Did another's actions or words cause a reaction in you? Then let that person free of your judgment; and unwrap the gift in the experience. It is for you, for your growth.

Lovingly,
River

Mantra for Today

February 23, 2021

In his extensive research and study, author, Bessel van der Kolk, offers great insight into physical manifestations of emotional stress in his book, The Body Keeps the Score: Brain, Mind, and Body in the Healing of Trauma. We are not our bodies, and we are intimately connected to the vessel we move in on earth. Chinese medicine has known this connection for 4 thousand years. Our difficulties or un-addressed struggles in life are neatly tucked away in our bodies, lying dormant until eventual activation, and present in the form of disease, or as we therapist term, dis-ease. This is inspiration to face the suppressed self-defeating thoughts and ideas, or conclusions made in early childhood and so forth, before they present as a physical problem. The body is a friend in the expression of the block, by bringing awareness. Pause and explore the message and begin to deal from the inside out.

Lovingly,
River

Mantra for Today

February 24, 2021

Find that still place within you and you have home. Inner turmoil comes from the mind interpretation. What we make a situation mean, concluding the intention of people in our lives, cause reaction. Reactions cause upset. The practice of centering yourself brings a stillness. From stillness we are effective. No matter what you must deal with, if you address it from anxious mind, it becomes catastrophic; if addressed from calmness it is easily handled. Somethings are simply observed, do nothing, somethings are approached skillfully. This brings effect change. Your true self awaits on the other side of distraction.

Lovingly,
River

Mantra for Today

February 25, 2021

In the fellowship of AA it is said that doing the same thing and expecting different results is the definition of insanity. When an old pattern of interaction with others is clearly not serving to the highest good of all involved, it is time to change. Change is daunting for most of us, especially when we have been unconsciously dancing to the beat of the drum we have been hypnotically programmed to from childhood. When change is called for, helpers rush in. Suddenly books with titles that nail the very concept calling for a change appear. People share in ways that resonate deeply. Change is a gradual patient process that begins with the tiny first step. We see what is not working and we committed to making the changes. We know it will not be easy, since old patterns are versed and automatic. With this in mind, we carefully plan for pitfalls and barriers, compassionately adjusting to setbacks and struggles. One day we realize, I am not that person anymore. I am more me, more whole, more complete. There is no one out there that can do this for you. Possibilities are abound!

Lovingly,
River

Mantra for Today

February 26, 2021

Sometimes, nothing can be done. When in anguish it is common to explore every causal factor in a situation. Why did a relationship slip? Everyone wants to be understood, seen and loved for exactly who they are, and sometimes that is impossible. The wounds of childhood manifested in traits that have become predominant behaviors. Self-protection interferes with trust and total surrender. Choosing an understanding of all aspects of the sad reality helps navigate the rough waters of what is. Caring for self by making the next moment better for oneself is what is called for now; don't over drink or eat or fall into negativity. Instead find the gift in it all, the personal growth and true change that is necessary for finding equanimity and wholeness.

Lovingly,
River

Mantra for Today

February 27, 2021

As we season in life, it is time to move out of identity claiming and survival mindset to shedding the ego self and thriving. Few humans reach full adulthood; clinging to stories of "who I was", rather than harvesting the gem of wisdom and letting go of the image of greatness. In the first phase of life, we need to establish ourselves as somebodies, programmed to get attention and be validated as worthy of a place on stage; thereby belonging. If in later life we still strive to declare, this is who I am, I am me, see me", we reveal a wounded part that is lost, still seeking place. To admit and attend to our wounds with humility and vulnerability we wake up to knowing ourselves from a witness standpoint. From here we can look with eyes unblinking and lovingly move ourselves into maturity, beyond surviving into thriving.

Lovingly,
River

Mantra for Today

February 28, 2021

When we were impressionable young children, we created meaning about ourselves and our roles in the world based on the environments we were raised in. For many of us childhood set the course of our interactions with others in a "survival" like dynamic. To not need or to be useful in order to be loved, for example, sets the stage for over functioning in a relationship and acquiescing to the sole needs of others. When we become aware of our unconscious source fracture story, (a term coined by Katherine Woodward Thomas), we can begin to relate with people in a more mutually fulfilling way, honoring ourselves and also the other. We are here to wake up, dear one, to unconscious patterns that at one time did serve to keep us alive but now we must shift out of those old worn out patterns and thrive!

Lovingly,
River

Mantra for Today

March 1, 2021

This or something better. As keen observers of change, we notice that life is a constant flow of shifts and changes. Technological changes in the past 50 years, a relatively short time frame, have taken us "from a rotary phone to a touch-tone or keypad phone, or even from a landline to a wireless phone, a disruptive technology displaces established assumptions, as in, say, combining a phone, a camera, a computer, a music library and player, a GPS device, and a mobile Internet portal." (Richard Rohr from the Center of Action and Contemplation.) We adapt to new situations after a brief resistance phase and eventually it becomes the new norm. The gift of change (hopefully)is growth and an expansion to greater expressions of love, acceptance and connection to truth. It is not easy to let go of long held attachments to identity and ego status. Once we wake up to see, the only threat is fear, a (fantasized experience appearing real), we can relax and trust in our abilities to flex and adapt. Motto for today, This or something better. Trusting in the source of all good we turn our challenges into our championship.

Lovingly,
River

Mantra for Today

March 2, 2021

Ego dictates that we control our environment, our interactions with others and protect our identity. We don't want conflict because it may expose our vulnerability and feelings might surface from the dungeon they have been exiled to. So, we ignore the invitation to an uncomfortable conversation. Better to defend self!, demands the ego, then release another from their anguish, long held hurts caused by refusal to hold audiences to another's pain. If a conversation would call the ego out and invite accountability, then, be damned, says the ego. The irony though is, a clearing conversation could bring freedom and greater connection than ever before. Honoring each and they speak out the pain and the hurt and the betrayal. This is just a human experience dear one, it is not who you are. When we clean up our side, we are free!

Lovingly,
River

Mantra for Today

March 3, 2021

There is a certain cycle all living being energetically move through. We strive for a fixed sense of certainty, yet nothing in the natural world is fixed or stable. We naturally go through a deconstruction or disorder from known to unknown. This is happening now, in this global pandemic. You may be experiencing disorder, change and uncertainty in your personal life as well. Everywhere there is disorder and uncertainty. Trust dear one, that what follows is a new order, a reconstruction, like a rebirthing of something more aligned with a higher purpose. Even though there may be a feeling of confusion and anxiety, as we breathe through the contractions, eventually it softens and there is ease again.

Lovingly,
River

Mantra for Today

March 4, 2021

Creating new agreements. Love is an experience of fullness and emptiness. We are hollowed out from the person we once were to the person we are becoming based on the great lessons and influential experiences that the relationship brought. When a relationship ends we naturally feel scorned, as the saying goes, hell hath no fury... once the anger has served its purpose, to generate the type of energy required to move forward, it's best to lay down the sword and accept life on life's terms. Rumi said, it seems like the end, it looks like a sunset but in reality it is the dawn. Wonder of wonders, it may be possible that your greatest potential is after the fall of your current idea of yourself. Everything in life is like a birthing process; we feel agony, we say no! We try to pretend this is not happening, we say, not now, not this, but the birth is in process. The best thing to do, the only thing, is to find the courage and commit to the birth and remember the gift at the end of this pain is precious new life.

Lovingly,
River

Mantra for Today

March 5, 2021

A dear soul was born on this day! We so not see things as they are, we see things as we are. Our projections onto the screen of what is, is based on our personal experiences, our feelings about ourselves and our general attitude. As we practice training the mind, we learn to stop thoughts that do not serve in bringing balance and contentment. We see and experience others and the world around us, in a much more accurate and inspiring way. With a trained mind, we see the previously flawed being as beautiful and whole. The mind will spin us to distraction if untrained. Peace and true seeing starts when the mind is used as a tool but never the master.

Lovingly,
River

Mantra for Today

March 6, 2021

We struggle when we lack skills. Communication, although in its purity, begins with good intentions, goes violently south without skillful means. Defensiveness begets defensiveness. Words are spoken that set the course into harmful places. Stop, dear ones, and listen to one another. Miracles happen when true seeing replaces fearful reactions. Love is a powerful tool when applied. Schools would do well to add communication to the curriculum. Here is a formula: listen without interruption, reflect what was heard, empathize and thank. This leads to reciprocity. The old way, blurt out hurt feelings, accuse and blame, interrupt and shout lead to violence and deep dissatisfaction. We are students of one another.

Lovingly,
River

Mantra for Today

March 7, 2021

The world appears to be wrapped up in debate dividing into various thoughts circles on politics, health and protocol. It is a time of awakening to the destructive nature of ego self. As we cling to our self-identity we cling to that which is changing, this is suffering. In Richard Rohr's Daily Meditation
From the Center for Action and Contemplation, he offers:

"If we do not let go of our separate /false self at the right time and in the right way, we remain stuck, trapped, and addicted. (The traditional word for that was sin.) Unfortunately, many people reach old age still entrenched in their egoic operating system. Only our True Self lives forever and is truly free in this world." Once we become clear, that our True Self is beyond the trappings of opinion, defensiveness, intolerance, beyond the divisive confines of the false ego self, we are at peace, we are free!

Lovingly,
River

Mantra for Today

March 8, 2021

To live separated from True Self is to be slave to constant performance. Until we can silence ourselves and step out of ego state we never fully contact the source of true seeing. Life challenges us and cracks us open, it's the only way we stop the delusion of control. We want to micro manage everything because we are insecure. We dread the thought of loss. This is what is meant in the Bible, ***"Whoever finds their life will lose it, and whoever loses their life for my sake will find it." - Matthew 10:39*** "for my sake" means for truth's sake. Losing the false self for the sake of authenticity. Until the peace is felt from moments of contact with who you really are is experienced directly, the illusion remains set in place, the doing self. Practice for today, be still.

Lovingly,
River

Mantra for Today

March 9, 2021

Every one of us is shadowed by an illusory person: a false self. This is the man I want myself to be but who cannot exist, because God does not know anything about him. And to be unknown of God is altogether too much privacy. —Thomas Merton

In our lives of personality, socially seen and assigned roles, we lose contact with our true nature. There is a time to retract and a time to expand. We know when to do which based on the energy felt. Mindfulness is a current practice in the modern world to presence oneself in felt energy. Access to truth through contemplation makes clear who I am vs who desire wants me to be. Today contact with spirit through stillness.

Lovingly,
River

Mantra for Today

March 10, 2021

Not everything that is faced can be changed; but nothing can be changed until it is faced. —James Baldwin (1924–1987

Conflict is part of every relationship. To be human is to error. When friction between people is not skillfully addressed, resentments build. With resentment comes stories or versions of perceived reality around the conflict. In couples work, the best skill is to listen for understanding, paraphrase what was heard, validate, giving the gift of non-judgment, and empathize, the gift of feeling intimately into the other person. The greatest insult to injury in relationship conflict is avoidance, passive aggressively making oneself unavailable to hold sacred space for clearing the hurt and suffering brought by conflict. In my experience, people repeat their grievances for years until they feel truly heard. Today, skillful listening.

Lovingly,
River

Mantra for Today

March 11, 2021

Where have we learned that punishment and harsh approaches bring favorable results? Childhood is rot with abuse at the hands of primary care givers. Children are verbally reprimanded, restrained and physically disciplined and yet behaviors are not corrected, they go covert at best. Why are we not raised with loving lessons of understanding and guidance? To persuade cooperation and train with lessons and natural consequences through means such as fables and loving compassion, would raise healthy minds and free spirits. Too many adults today are reactive beings, dysfunctional and rebellious. Today, reparenting self through ceremony of reclaiming childhood, committing to nonviolence towards self or other. Experiment today with seeing results from kind approaches verses the automatic reaction of punitive intentions.

Lovingly,
River

Mantra for Today

March 12, 2021

True empowerment is owning your experience. Self-accountability is more than responsibility, it is committing to personal growth through the emotional reactions stimulated by relationships. Whenever we blame the other, we give away our dignity, we reduce ourselves to victims. Moving through life in this way is to be stuck in childhood. Inner work is healing work. On this trajectory, we make ourselves available to relationships. We come to the relationship whole, willing to collaborate. No greater hell is there than living at the mercy of trigger reactions. Put down your defenses and go within. Here you will find your pure precious self-waiting for your compassion and release from the personal prison of illusionary victimization. Today, notice all the ways the finger is pointed at other and turn it towards self; not to blame self but to lovingly take the reins and heal the barriers to clear understanding.

Lovingly,
River

Mantra for Today

March 13, 2021

As we sojourn through the earthly plane, we are accompanied by many helpers and guides. These helpers come in many forms. An animal helper touches us deeply in places no human relationship can. We always get exactly who and what we need. When we see everything as a gift for our passage, all is experienced as grace. Today, see the amazing gem in everything; in the joy of connection and in the pain of loss. Everything is a gift for our highest good. My loving presence is with you dear one.

Lovingly,
River

Mantra for Today

March 14, 2021

Habitual turning to the mind for information is reflexive. We know on some level that we are spiritual beings living in human form; and that the human form is riddled with fears, doubts, and scarcity. The spiritual Self, knows all beings are rich with abundance of love and peace and that we are free. Habitually we operate from the human personality, even though this approach brings suffering. We create a bondage scenario out of habit. Most of us are dragging ourselves out of trauma which imprinted on us limitations. Spirit knows no human experience is purely damaging, but are for our human evolution. This may show as compassion, non identification, or the understanding that we are here to do a certain thing, evolve. Non identification is the main aim. Have compassion and understanding when disheartened by another's view of you. It is the human mind's Interpretation based on fears. The human dynamic is a set up for delusional versions of reality; love becomes stained by reactionary patterns based on conditioning. When we observe from spirit, we know that people are not behaving from love not because we don't love but because we forgot who they are.

Lovingly,
River

Mantra for Today

March 15, 2021

We live our greatest potential when we give up the fight. Peaceful beings stand on the foundation of choosing to let the grievances go. I believe that people act unconsciously when wounds of their past are unresolved. Talk therapy, therefore, is a sacred conversation where hurts are heard, and counsel is offered. New insights and ways of seeing and thinking resource us in participating in ways that create peace. There are many indigenous traditions that support this method of healing. Talking circles with elders where a structured process holds individuals accountable and restores connection. Today seek ways of restoring connection with people.

Lovingly,
River

Mantra for Today

March 16, 2021

The path of relationship is a spiritual discourse of epic self-advantage. When we go the distance with people by staying the course through difficult conversations and challenging encounters, personal growth is exponential. Avoidance is postponement. When people develop the type of interpersonal skills that result in mutual satisfying interactions, there is joy immeasurable. Today practice being in-tune with feelings, authentically reveal your minds made up story, seek what is truer, and reach for the mutual goal of understanding as being understood.

Lovingly,
River

Mantra for Today

March 17, 2021

Religion has been the cause of great division, shame, manipulation, guilt, war, righteous judgment and "power over" tactics, to name but a few harmful effects. Religious institutions have mandates for exclusivity. Many are rejecting dogma and liturgical following and remaining spiritually attuned with deep values of integrity and living truth. Every tribe, nation and culture around the world has truth traditions expressed in manners of life style, folklore and traditions. One truth expressed in many ways. Truth is truth, how could it be otherwise? So regardless of the title, word or name given to the teacher, truth is the source. Words are like little cages with meaning its prisoner. When we touch inward for our own direct relationship with truth, we become the authors of our own narrative that speaks to our own understanding. For me, my God, is Love, for me everything is sourced from love, I let love guide my thoughts and actions.

Lovingly,
River

Mantra for Today

March 18, 2021

As we sojourn through the earthly plane, we are accompanied by many helpers and guides. These helpers come in many forms. An animal helper touches us deeply in places no human relationship can. We always get exactly who and what we need. When we see everything as a gift for our passage, all is experienced as grace. Today, see the amazing gem in everything; in the joy of connection and in the pain of loss. Everything is a gift for our highest good. My loving presence is with you dear one.

Lovingly,
River

Mantra for Today

March 19, 2021

Mantra for Today The recent presidential debate reveals that the core value of men in power is to power over one another and to be seen as dominate. There appears to be no shame in this behavior as it is publicly broadcast across the nation for all to see. A very masculine puffing of feathers and snorting before aggressive charge. The ego driven governance has brought great harm to societies in times gone by, why do we still give it stage and audience? Emotional sobriety and humble service to humanity is a faint and foreign construct in our political times. Today, despite the models before us, be the peaceful negotiator and selfless servant of the greater good for all involved; look to examples such as Saint Francis instead of broadcast news.

Lovingly,
River

Mantra for Today

March 20, 2021

There is soul in everything. As I participated in a web summit called A Magnificent New Normal, Lynne Twist spoke of her walk in the Amazon with a shaman who turned to her, took her hand and asked, can you hear the souls? He was hearing the souls of every manner of species all around. St. Francis of Assisi, learned by his connection to nature that everything natural is loved by the creator, just as is! Simple and free, this includes us! Our true mother is Mother Earth, our true father is Father Sky, we all belong. Today, presence. Still the mind of stories of epic life events and be one with all life. I love you totally!

Lovingly,
River

Mantra for Today

March 21, 2021

What we permit, we promote. When as individuals we turn a blind eye to minor infractions, racial slurs, harsh treatment of animals or children believing it is not our business, we silently validate a belief that we are powerless against the forces of anger and hatred among us. Many of us have learned to be passive based on fear of judgment or exile. Passivity on a larger scale allows nation states, institutions and corporations to have unbounded reign regardless of breaking moral and ethical codes upheld by the general population. Today, be in tune with your values and from there precent your walk-in life. What are you standing for? What can you no longer stand? Where do you take a stand? Your contribution makes a difference, respond without love and let the cards land as they land.

Lovingly,
River

Mantra for Today

March 22, 2021

I am you and you are me. It is false to think anything is happening to you; what is happening, is happening for us. We are not separate, humanity, animals and birds and insects, all inter connect. What is expressed through one, vibrationally impacts all living beings. It is a false belief to think you are alone. Your hurt is my hurt, your joy is mine; we are reflections always. When you need love, give love, when you have a windfall, share. Loving others is loving yourself. Today, see in others yourself, tune in to what is needed in you and receive it through giving.

Lovingly,
River

Mantra for Today

March 23, 2021

All suffering comes from the mind. There is such a thing as sickness without suffering. I have personally enjoyed the company of individuals going through health challenges with joy and happiness. It is when we fuse our ideas of ourselves, and images of identity with certain states, such as health, that we are susceptible to suffering. We are far greater than our health, far greater than our addictions, far greater than our behaviors. All of these are results of thoughts and beliefs. We are not guilty of thoughts; we are not to blame for our state. We simply forgot who we truly are. My teacher, Mooji, encourages us to use "mind attacks", as opportunity to see where we are still attached to an identity of self. Remembering who you are brings a neutral witness to all states without suffering or judgment. From this loving place we can change. My loving support is with you!

Lovingly,
River

Mantra for Today

March 24, 2021

The old ways are no longer working; a new way is called for. As we face the reality that our tried and true responses to life no longer bring results, we are faced with luminal space. It is uncomfortable and disorientating to not know what to do or how to be, now that the old patterns are dull and ineffectual. This is a time silence and compassion. In the still place of not knowing, there is opportunity for clarity and choice. Today: stand on your foundation of values; from kindness, fairness, loving compassion make your next move.

Lovingly,
River

Mantra for Today

March 25, 2021

When we strive for happiness by focusing on external symbols, we are mystified by dissatisfaction. The right body, the right clothing, the house and partner, the children and pets none in themselves can bring happiness. When we take full responsibility for our own thoughts, feelings and behaviors and realize which align with our values; then we begin to choose the direction of our lives. Happiness may or may not be a byproduct; if we are at peace with ourselves from the inside out, there is the greatest gift.

Lovingly,
River

Mantra for Today

March 26, 2021

As spirits living in human form we do not die. Our bodies do but then life essence remains. That energy can be felt when we empty ourselves of mind, stories, attachments and desires. It is the minds clinging, wanting, expecting that rises in us a sense of catastrophe horror and no good no good. Still yourself dear one, notice within you that energetic vibration that is without form, without name or face or body. That is, you! The true you! Everything else is personhood, script, drama, cultural belief and social influence. Drop inward for your anchor. This is where peace awaits. Today I accept life as is and allow the unfolding of events without labels. I drop into my core essential cord, which is my truth, there I am always home.

Lovingly,
River

Mantra for Today

March 27, 2021

As we travel forward in life fully awake, we notice shifts. Resisting nothing means witness from a place of non-judgment. See what is happening without clinging to wanting or refusing to accept, we are free. Recognize yourself, not the face in the mirror but the formless Self that lives in the form in the mirror. Your form is not you; your beauty is your love. It is far easier to be your true self than it is to be your sculpted actor memorizing scripts of proper social conduct. Today practice stilling that busy mind and see from the position of neutral observing. Love guides.

Lovingly,
River

Mantra for Today

March 28, 2021

Spiritual teacher, Ram Dass left his body on December 22, 2019. In the spiritual community this is the language used to describe what mainstream society calls death. The animated force within a life, has been described by certain religions as capable of traveling to heaven or to hell based on choices. Certain atheists believe after this life, death means dead, gone, no more period. Ram Dass was a Harvard professor of psychology and midlife became a devote of a Hindu practice. The teaching suggests our bodies are form and our life force is formless. That which never dies is who we are. Leaving the body, although sad since our beloved is no longer here to be with in physical form, is joyous because now they have graduated from form and are free of form. Consider who you are beyond your body. Notice that accompanying voice, called mind, and think beyond mind, who are you? Today, I will sit with this question and get a little space around me and my body and my mind and observe what and who I am.

Lovingly,
River

Mantra for Today

March 29, 2021

There are those among us who are taking personal accountability for their thought's feelings and actions. These are people who, by addressing negative thinking create and promote peaceful environments. We trust them to resolve their judgments and maintain balance. Currently, this last week we bore witness to what happens when hateful fearful thinking becomes popular. The world is at the threat of war. When does war solve anything? When does military presence inspire peace? Peace begins with you dear one. In your circle, stop projecting negative assumptions or lies about your personal value on earth. You are the possibility of peace in your microcosm. You make the difference. Today, I increase my focus on loving myself and others, animals and humans alike and I will be the change I wish to see in the world.

Lovingly,
River

Mantra for Today

March 30, 2021

We are swimming in grace, the mind makes us doubt. Sadness clouds in like a London fog when a thought of lack comes in. Do others love me as much as I love them? Is there something, which I am unaware of, that makes me particularly unlikeable? Maybe I'm too much for people or maybe I'm not enough of the right stuff. All this dear one, comes from mind. We are essentially love, then fear, scarcity and doubt reduce the felt experience. Seeking love from an external person feeds the insecurity. Who would you be if you knew you were abundantly loved, lovable and loving? Who would you be without your little and big fears? Today, this new day, I will take off the cloak of mind-numbing chatter and be in this moment aware of my divine place in the world, love.

Lovingly,
River

Mantra for Today

March 31, 2021

Most of us prefer to push away uncomfortable feelings and move on. There is a tendency to mask how we feel to prevent reactions from other people. Some of us have been parented to not cry or not show anger. Recognizing the feeling without judgment, allowing yourself to feel it, investigate where it stems from and nurture yourself through the process is what Tara Brach coined R.A.I.N. Today I will develop a healthy relationship with the energy in emotions rather than suppress them. This will make a difference. I will no longer carry charges emotions I will experience them and be complete again.

Lovingly,
River

Mantra for Today

April 1, 2021

Spiritual teacher, Mooji teaches, if we begin to meditate still attached to our stories, we sit with the mind. The past comes in; memories come reviewing and rehashing events, plans for the future also come up and we begin making lists, we sit in total distraction. When we leave our cushion, we are no more grounded then when we sat down. Visualize, as you begin your meditation, that you are taking off your shoes before entering a sacred space. Take off your past and future as well and leave that at the door. Now sit dear one, in the empty space with your Self. Remember who you are without the scripts and reels of all that has been projected upon your screen of identity and be in the space of stillness. From here, life becomes seen through a clearer lens.

Lovingly,
River

Mantra for Today

April 2, 2021

Good Friday, in the Christian tradition is the day that Jesus was sacrificed on the cross, so that the people could find redemption from their harmful nature. This notion of humans as born in sin might be translated as, we humans have a tendency towards fear. Fear leads us to react, often naive to the effects on others. I was raised in a very strict Christian household, I learned that I needed to be a constant sacrifice in order to be loved. If I view the crucifixion as a model of recognition of my human proclivities and self-forgiveness, my prayer is: may I be accountable when I error, may I forgive myself and others, may I live present in the awareness of the continuous flow of grace. Regardless of your beliefs, there is a message in all spiritual traditions that can apply to us all. None of us are perfect, we must die to our negative patterns, and be resurrected anew each day through grace. The force that makes this possible is love. Today the example presents in our Western religion is forgiveness. To quote my favorite poem, Wild Geese, by Mary Oliver: "You do not have to be good. You do not have to walk on your knees for a hundred miles through the desert repenting..." When I fell in love, I surrendered a part of myself to the beloved. I gave a bit of myself away to love, I surrendered my autonomy and included another's wellbeing and life's story into my field of interest. I expanded into a larger reality. As I am experiencing, with the rest of the world, the Covid pandemic crisis, I am learning, I have little control. I must surrender to the divine flow of things. Surrendering to love is choosing to die to myself. The story of Jesus, as we approach good Friday, shows how he washed others feet, counselled people to forgive one another, and finally showed the people how to trust in a greater outcome no matter how devastating it feels; when no matter your intentions you are nailed to the cross, you have no control of your circumstances. As we surrender to what is, we "pass over" our privilege, our need to control and our power to a higher order. It is uncomfortable to live in uncertain times dear one, resist nothing. Be in harmony with what wants to happen with curiosity and willingness. Stay present moment oriented, the future will unfold as it does, you are loved.

Lovingly,
River

Mantra for Today

April 3, 2021

Every relationship is a learning experience. How we react to the stimulus is an open book titled What's Alive in Me. Personal accountability for our own reactions points us directly to our values, our sensitivities and our undeveloped bits. If we take the magnifying glass off the other person and focus our gaze at ourselves, a rich opportunity awaits. Doing inner work with another need not be painful. Choose a partner that does not traumatize you. The shock of insult and injury may make the personal growth go a little slower since the pain may be too blinding. Choose instead a partner who is willing to lovingly process the triggers, quirks and old habits of reaction in a space of safe exploration. Today I will commit to myself to remain emotionally safe. I will walk away from abuse and attack and take space to nurture myself.

Lovingly,
River

Mantra for Today

April 4, 2021

Easter

Mantra for Today In keeping with theme of death and resurrection, it is important to become still and reflect on the principles that support you. A religion, belief system or spiritual path isn't worth a lick if it doesn't bring comfort in times of trial. In the world we live in there are many choices of spirituality to guide and support the journey. As we face the duality of new love with hopes and dreams and the gradual broken heart of dashed agreements, or good health and the eventual decline, or gainful employment and the down turn of the economy, with some sort of resilience we are grounded in a restful state taking stock and bearing the darkness. Our spirit selves know there is a silver lining in every dark cloud. Be still and allow the truth to reveal what is evident reality, bear it with grace and be present for something better. Now is our opportunity dear one.

Lovingly,
River

Mantra for Today

April 5, 2021

Being informed about what is happening in the world can be both expansive and deeply disappointing. Human greed has been the impetus of vast cruelty. We may feel that as an individual we have no voice nor influence over big business and collective unconscious. This belief slips us into inertia and helplessness. This, dear one, may be a source of depression. Susan Casey, author of, Voices in the Ocean, is a Maui resident who has been one individual who has taken the initiative as an individual to speak, through her writing, exposing the plights of our fellow planet dwellers, the dolphins. We don't know until we know that actions are harming another species who have been studied and shown high levels of empathy, compassion and social intelligence equal (if not superior) to humans. Today, I will tap into my personal responsibility to be the change needed to support and protect others from the hand of my brothers and sister around the world.

Lovingly,
River

Mantra for Today

April 6, 2021

Life is beautiful. We often don't see the beauty all around us. Caught up in imaginary fears and mental doubts seem so convincing that life is hard and painful. We are caught up in the illusion of struggle. Meanwhile, beauty is there all the while. We seek what is within us as though it is something to earn or learn or attain. Stepping through the fog of delusion, it is simply right here. Removing the obstructions made from mind we realize; we are not going through hard times it is going through us. There is nothing to do. Be still and awaken to beauty, peace and pure joy in grace. Today, I will be with what is all around me.

Lovingly,
River

Mantra for Today

April 7, 2021

Those who have been addicted to a substance and then have had some time in recovery know something clearly. Actions taken while actively using violate values, morals and tainted their sense of identity. While sober, they show responsibility, create connections, and move in the world respectfully. At some point living clean is far more attractive and has more rewarding outcomes that even imagining going back to old habits bring disgust. Today, I am whelmed with gratitude for clear seeing of these two options of living, and humbly and mindfully make every step a prayer and every word, a word of love.

Lovingly,
River

Mantra for Today

April 8, 2021

Are you sick? This is what is one everybody's mind right now. If you are physically well, yet you are anxious and fearful, you are missing the benefit of wellness. We cannot control the outside world of viruses and restrictions, but what is in our control is the inner life, our adaptability and choice of response. To support yourself, take up meditation and listen to something inspiring on You Tube or some other means of spiritual influence. Use this time and all challenging experiences to deepen your practice of inner evolution. Otherwise you are spinning your wheels and are stuck in suffering. You can do this dear one, I know this because you have incarnated on a magnificent human journey. Life is one big opportunity to practice witnessing and responding from a place of peaceful adaptability.

Lovingly,
River

Mantra for Today

April 9, 2021

The mind can be very convincing. Nit-picky little negative complaints can permeate a situation or relationship clouding out the positive. Once it starts it can go rogue. Like a finding monster, it attacks self, other, past and future. Even though it all seems so real, catch yourself dear one. Stop allowing the mind to reign your empire. Become present to what else is true. Notice the good, remember the gifts of life. Drop into gratitude and steer yourself back onto right thinking and right action. The present moment offers the possibility of awe and wonder for all the good you have attracted. Be with this today.

Lovingly,
River

Mantra for Today

April 10, 2021

Fear is imaging a worst-case scenario that may never come to pass, but the effects are happening non the less. Believe it or not, there is an element of choice even in a fearful moment. Some of our fears come from a real event which occurred in the past. It was real and it was terrifying, catastrophic and bad. Yet, when the past is projected upon a current situation that resembles the past one, it doesn't necessarily translate to the same. The ironic thing is, fear itself can cause an otherwise innocent moment into the exact same past experience. The choice is practicing "not knowing already". Remember who you are today is far more resourced possibility because of your past traumas. Using conscious awareness, you can change your energy field and relax in the face of a challenge. From here you are empowered. Today, I will stop terrifying myself and empower myself with my life's experiences.

Lovingly,
River

Mantra for Today

April 11, 2021

Life has its way of showing us just where we are needing to place our attention. Change of routine can be imposed by a sudden injury or illness. When we resist what is so, we struggle. When we say, "No not this", we are wrestle with reality. There is grace in the benevolent universe. When we look beneath our circumstances, we see we are supported in our situation. It is here, when we surrender that we are softened. Today, I will ask for what I need and love my life exactly as it is. I am loved, I can rest knowing everything is exactly as it should be.

Lovingly,
River

Mantra for Today

April 12, 2021

Expectations impose imaginary frames onto people, situations and self which block clear seeing of what is. We tell ourselves; I'm not getting what I want. It should be this other way. Comparisons come up and we start to feel deep dissatisfaction. It could be equally true that what we have is exactly perfect compared to some other relationship, situation or way of life. Again, the mind interferes and shades a bright light, dimming the perception. This is where meditation helps. Being still with yourself, separating from the demands of perceptions, thoughts, emotions and feelings and breath. In this space there is emptiness. Here there is no problem. We eventually unhook from our small self-complaints and just are. Today I will practice meditation, a little space brings forth much ease.

Lovingly,
River

Mantra for Today

April 13, 2021

Truly loving we or another is accepting as is. Loving self or other with parameters of some ideal, keeps us in duplicity. We feel we must be good in order to be lovable, so we fake our happiness or spirituality. When we disallow our humanity, we create this unattainable image of who a lovable person is like. Dropping all ideas of perfection, we simply allow and acknowledge our real time experience from an observer's stand point. This allowing and accepting of ourselves and others in our humanness is freedom. Letting go of posturing perfection we can relax. Today I love myself and others as we are.

Lovingly,
River

Mantra for Today

April 14, 2021

The feeling of separateness is at the causal point of picking up. We humans forget we are all connected, we are never alone, but the feelings of being separate is so unbearable that we reach for a drug, or a drink or sex to feel connected, albeit brief. When we remember we are embraced by life and are interconnected with all life, and that our life matters, we can put it down and become present. Today I will be mindful of truth and beauty and love all around me.

Lovingly,
River

Mantra for Today

April 15, 2021

Learning to communicate effectively liberates. So much confusion happens when we speak unskillful. Directness and truth are refreshing in a world of people pleasing insufferable biting of tongue, however, when spoken without kindness it goes unheard. It is never too late to learn the language of truth spoken from a place of loving kindness. This is a learned skill for many. Once practiced the results are amazing. No need for apology, no need for regret, words spoken brought about change, or affirmed or rebutted delivered skillfully. This is non-violence. Today, I will learn to address my world with right intention, purposefully and kindly.

Lovingly,
River

Mantra for Today

April 16, 2021

Become comfortable with discomfort. Avoiding discomfort, we try to please people, we drink or drug or seek release in other ways. When we get that we are in human form to transcend our fears, insecurities and doubt we welcome life's lessons, even when uncomfortable. That annoying person who spoke ill of you, that mirror that reflects unhealthy lifestyle, that reminder of a time that was hurtful, all of this is opportunity to transcend towards freedom. Stand before the discomfort and let go of the story. Be with it, endure it while, what is true becomes clearer. Take courage dear one, it is all in your path for your liberation. Imagine how good it will feel to no longer have a charge in direct experience with that familiar trigger!

Lovingly,
River

Mantra for Today

April 17, 2021

When a significant relationship becomes clearly impossible to continue it feels like the world is crashing all around you. Everything known feels like deception, every word now in question. In times like these grounds yourself in truth. Know that your safe place is inner peace. Distraction only serves to keep you temporarily focused elsewhere, the reality of what's happening is still there. Amp up yourself care dear one. Refuse drugs and alcohol and over eating. Walk off the disappointment. Sit still with music that soothe the soul, talk as much as you need to loving people and gently you move towards acceptance. Know that how you act in strife will leave you feeling worse or better. Choose actions and responses that you will look back on and be satisfied with. My loving support is with you,

Lovingly,
River

Mantra for Today

April 18, 2021

"I want to sing like the birds sing, not worrying about who hears or what they think." -Rumi

When we are hurt by others, or by our circumstances, it may seem like the world is ending. But, it is in these moments when we are wounded that we find our courage, our strength, and we develop the character that takes us closer to our truest self. In all you do, absolutely everything. Let love be the core. Let love be the essence. Lean into love, dear one. Live life for you. Sing your song and dance happily to your own drum. Joy and happiness are meant for you too, without paying painful costs for admission. Today, know that you are worthy.

Lovingly,
River

Mantra for Today

April 19, 2021

Anam Cara: "your heart and my heart are very, very old friends." A friendship is a loved one who awakens your life in order to free the many wild possibilities that flourish in you. The one you love, your anam cara, your soul friend, is the truest mirror to reflect your soul. The honesty and clarity of true friendship also brings out the real depth of your spirit; always accepting the possibilities of who you are, who you want to become. Today you are understood, you are at home, you belong, my love.

Lovingly,
River

Mantra for Today

April 20, 2021

Wendell Berry captures why walking into solitude, despite its discomforts, is the basis for cultivating our connection with the world. "Always in big woods when you leave familiar ground and step off alone into a new place there will be, along with the feelings of curiosity and excitement, a little nagging of dread. It is the ancient fear of the unknown, and it is your first bond with the wilderness you are going into," he writes. "You are undertaking the first experience, not of the place, but of yourself in that place. It is an experience of our essential loneliness, for nobody can discover the world for anybody else. It is only after we have discovered it for ourselves that it becomes a common ground and a common bond, and we cease to be alone.

Lovingly,
River

Mantra for Today

April 21, 2021

To be wise is to process life's experiences. So, few people were actually counselled to do this, this is why we have such few true elders among us.

Processing old age through the lens of ego losses; the body, mental capacity and virility, these people become bitter, complaining and alone. We read books and study and have intelligence, but this is not wisdom. Wisdom comes from harvesting the lesson of how to love and how to let love in. Process your life dear one. Spend time with a therapist or willingly open up to feedback. As we edge towards leaving our earthly body, make your final years your swan song, the best possible.

Lovingly,
River

Mantra for Today

April 22, 2021

Today's message is inspired by Richard Rore. "The intellectual center is a profoundly useful tool for exploring and navigating the world, and it allows us to do things that separate us from the rest of the animals. But the program it runs is perception through separation. It's a grand separating, evaluating, and measuring tool. It can't ask two questions: "Who am I, and who is God?" because these questions can't be measured by an operating system that depends on separation. I have sometimes said that doing the journey toward mystical union with the mind is like trying to play the violin with a chainsaw. It's not that the chainsaw is bad, but its nature is to cut and not make music.

The emotional center is the capacity to explore and receive information from the world through empathetic entrainment by what we might call vibrational resonance, It is our antenna, so to speak, given to us to orient us toward the divine radiance. The heart is not for personal expression but for divine perception.
Today I will balance, to be whole.

Lovingly,
River

Mantra for Today

April 23, 2021

When we stop resisting reality and put all the cards face up on the table, real freedom comes. There are myriad ways of relating. Traditional marriage can be stifling, each individual is constantly evolving and expanding to be who they were born to be. When I come from a deeper, steadier, and quieter place in my heart and mind, I celebrate the unfolding and dance joyfully for myself and my beloved. Today I let it all wash to shore and get my feet wet and dance. There are no catastrophes only possibilities.

Lovingly,
River

Mantra for Today

April 24, 2021

We don't know until we know. Innocently or ignorantly we engage and commit with high ideals when the heart urns for belonging. Few of us have experienced true belonging as children. We childlike ones reach for companionship, for home for identity, we need to be cherished so that we can know ourselves. The denied emotions of childhood lay suppressed, we haven't learned how to express, the cost, authenticity. No relationship can survive inauthenticity. So, the search begins again. Like the book, Chicken Little, we ask, "Are you my mother?", to any animated object. Inner work is remembering who you are. Once you find yourself, any place is home.

Lovingly,
River

Mantra for Today

April 25, 2021

Today is the first day of the rest of your life. The mind and ego act as "handlers" of life; dictating thoughts leading to feelings and resentments. The heart is the center of truth as we stop our automatic distractions and be with what is. Truth may feel painful, as our love interest speaks from a less than kind place, the mind defends, blames and narratives a victim's song. All this angst and suffering must lead to some unrevealed false belief. Perhaps, "I am loved and belong only if I am perfect". Not so! dear one! You don't have to prove your worth. Be in present moment awareness of what is and move there with self-love and love for all beings. This is your super power.

Lovingly,
River

Mantra for Today

April 26, 2021

"Wisdom is not the result of mental effort. It cannot be gained through intellectual study. Even life experiences do not make us wise if we don't process them humbly and consciously". Richard Rohr

Processing childhood trauma is not merely self-indulgence and navel gazing. It is imperative in order to grow to become fully mature. Untreated trauma manifests in identify confusion, repressed self-expression and a sense of being an alien on earth. Find someone who you can delve deep with dear one. A beloved partner who can hold space for excavations of things buried alive in you. A skillful therapist that knows how to love you to the other side is helpful. Wisdom comes with working through the unresolved past. Many older folks never arrive at wisdom because avoidance has been their main practice in dealing with emotional pain. It only gets better through process; we are all works of process!

Lovingly,
River

Mantra for Today

April 27, 2021

Marion Woodman wrote, "Children not loved for who they are do not learn how to love themselves. Their growth is an exercise in pleasing others, not in expanding through experience." Real love requires us to expose our wounded parts and surrender our defenses. If we haven't learned to love ourselves we avoid true intimacy and become addicted to work or other distractions that gain us approval but keep our true selves behind closed doors. To break free of these patterns of behavior in relationship to one self and others, we must learn to inquire within. Getting InTouch with feelings and emotions and beliefs and becoming honest with what is alive in us. Pause for a moment dear one and speak or write what your direct experience is in this moment. See what wants your attention. See what you are resisting. It is never too late to retrieve the lost child within and bring up to date the wounded parts. In loving ourselves for who we are, our intelligence, sexuality, characteristics, personal preferences, needs and wants, we begin to stand on solid ground. As we become honest with ourselves we live authentically.

Lovingly,
River

Mantra for Today

April 28, 2021

When you were a baby, beyond the need for nourishment and shelter, you had a fundamental need to be gazed at by a loving mother. Her eyes seeing you, attuned to your magnificence you would have a sense of who you are through the mirrors of her eyes. If this was not your experience, you likely dwell with shame running in the dark recesses of your psyche. Psychologist, Carl Jung described shame as "a soul-eating emotion. Shame, like a master, leaves us slave to a state of "obligation to our wounding mothers--to keep pleasing or achieving, remain stoic, unconscious, or angry. We can't imagine what life would be like without shame because in a twisted sense it has been a kind of caretaker to us. Shame leads us to the defenses that we mistakenly believe will protect or comfort us. It becomes part of our self-concept.

It's important to add here that these defenses probably have protected us or comforted us along the way. As children, we needed to disappear into our imaginations or become stoic in order to learn to meet our own needs, in order to cope and survive." (Daily Om; The Mother Wound). The healing begins when we retrieve our wounded child and become that caring loving mother. If you are able to receive this loving gaze from a trusted friend or therapist practice compassionately letting your child part feel this deep reverence of your divinity dear one. Remember you are a spiritual being having a human experience, it is your homework to heal.

Lovingly,
River

Mantra for Today

April 29, 2021

If we don't change, we don't grow. If we don't grow, we aren't really living. -Gail Sheehy

It is often said that change is the only constant in life. Yet us humans are evolutionarily predisposed to resist change because of the risk associated with it - the possible gains or losses. Despite this resistance to change, it is more important than ever. In current society the pace of change is faster, and it will only continue to accelerate. It seems that the only option is to hop on the train, or get left behind, stuck, inauthentic, unhappy. The ones that don't embrace change are bound to lose ground and stagnate. While you are anxiously anticipating change or in the midst of a challenging one, remember my love, you are amazingly beautiful just the way you are! Today hold your head high, and keep plowing through, there's a pot of gold at the end of each and every rainbow.

Lovingly,
River

Mantra for Today

April 30, 2021

Forgiveness is the necessary practice towards true freedom. When we hold resentments from the past, we carry a certain burden deep within. Forgiveness doesn't mean we no longer hold the other person accountable for their actions, nor do we condone their behavior. Instead, forgiveness is cutting the cord of vibrations between the two of you. It doesn't mean you now go to full trust; no, we learn to use discernment. Forgiveness is a spiritual practice; seeing the other person's actions as their wounded self. There is a divine pure and loving being within the wounded reactive part. Forgiveness is knowing that part exists while at the same time giving yourself some space from the part in that person which harmed you. Forgiveness takes time, begin the process by feeling the emotions within you, understand where the hurtful acts stem from and lovingly commit to self-care. All this applies to self-forgiveness as well, precious.

Lovingly,
River

Mantra for Today

May 1, 2021

Learning to communicate directly creates closeness and prevents misunderstandings, hurt feelings and resentments. When we believe our feelings are wrong, we may adopt a stoic stance to prevent exposing those feelings. There are no wrong emotions, emotions are energy in motion, they wave in and out; so long as we do no harm. Sometimes feelings point to something that needs our attention. Better to examine feelings than to suppress them. Many of us engage in passive aggressive behavior. This means suppressing our true feelings and portraying what we think is a less confrontational stance. In the world of psychology, this is a disordered way of being. It is inauthentic and leads to confusion, dissatisfaction and ultimately disconnection in relationships. Many of us are conflict phonics, ironically however, by pretending to be fine when we are uncomfortable leads to conflict which eats away the relationship like rust. Beginning today, be truthful and clear in communication and reap the rewards of authenticity. All cards face up on the table.

Lovingly,
River

Mantra for Today

May 2, 2021

Being seen and acknowledged for something we've done instead of for who we are creates an identity of worth through productivity. The accolades and admiration for the outcome of our creativity or service lands lightly because we've become conditioned to see ourselves as valuable only when we do something. It is important to embrace those friends and loved ones who are eagerly showing us our value is in our simple presence, in the miracle of our existence ; and all the doing is bonus but not necessarily in order to be loved. Brainwashed into thinking our success in "doing" defines us, aging folk become depressed, feel worthless and a burden when the doing part expires. Aging gracefully means loving yourself and opening your heart to loving others. Walk in love dear one, love is right there in you as your natural attraction.

Lovingly,
River

Mantra for Today

May 3, 2021

Today's mantra is about love. 1st Corinthians 13 describes love thus: Love is patient, love is kind. It does not envy, it does not boast, it is not proud, it is not rude, it is not self-seeking, it is not easily angered, it keeps no record of wrongs. Love does not delight in evil but rejoices with the truth. It always protects, always trusts, always hopes, always perseveres. It is heart wrenching when those who previously professed to love one another, made promises to one another to protect and care for one another, then turn hatred towards that very love interest. I say that was not love in the first place but was an arrangement for serving the ego. What shines brightly is the realm of love is that even though and especially when things get tricky, individuals rise beyond their egos and are great personally and spiritually. Today I choose accountability for my actions and override the wounded ego and shine the love that is me.

Lovingly,
River

Mantra for Today

May 4, 2021

When we are children, we learn that in order to have freedom we must behave. This programming sets the stage for a life time of belief that our value is dependent on the positive regard of others. The word persona refers to the mask or facade that shields or hides aspects we have learned are not cherished by people close to us. A spiritual practice gets us in touch with our true nature, our authenticity, freeing us to discover our true identity and our own heart's desire. Uncovering our truth, we clear the blocks that keep us shut down and isolated in our dark private minds. This is where deviance seeps out to release the pressure of being good in order to be loved. Still your mind dear one and tune into the genuine reality of your divine being, and from there move into living life, unapologetically you.

Lovingly,
River

Mantra for Today

May 5, 2021

We human beings are complex to say the least. I choose to believe that at the core we are all divine and that a possibility exists in us all to be equanimous, loving and fair. When we are out of balance however, and out of touch with our true selves, we can become paranoid defended and vengeful. No one is exempt from dualism. It has been my experience that my life fairs better when I respond from a balanced healthy state. When hurt and fear lead, destruction touches not only the object of attack but every aspect of one's own life as well. Find your center dear one. Return to your spirit self and choose to navigate from love and fairness. My loving support is with you always.

Lovingly,
River

Mantra for Today

May 6, 2021

Let everything happen to you;
Beauty and terror
Just keep going,
No feeling is final.
~Rainer Maria Rilke

Everything is unfolding exactly as it should. We humans are one of the natural worlds. Like butterflies and dinosaurs, we too are affected by climate, pressures, food choices and airborne viruses. Fear not the future, for you do not know what is to come. Fear is like asking to experience now what you don't want. Instead, be the best human you can be. Slow down and take inventory of your life. Are you having the conversations that inspire yourself and the listener? Are you softening the world for yourself and others through kindness? Now is the time to put aside grievances' and held resentments and move more consciousness than ever before. What we have now is an opportunity to be great, wise and the highest potential for love. Everything is exactly as it should be, and we are blessed.

Lovingly,
River

Mantra for Today

May 7, 2021

The practice of conscious present moment awareness is essential regarding challenging and changing times. I recently became present to an aspect of myself that surfaced for healing when an innocent individual behaved in ways that seemed out of tune and downright ignorant. Stressed, under fed and sleep deprived, I was aghast and frustrated and hurt by this person's level of naivety and reacted as though it was being done on purpose. We humans are informed and react through the lens of our own temperament, early conditioning, brain function, role and place in society, education, our personal needs, cultural biases and assumptions. Soon after, what I felt and thought of as an assault, I gained greater understanding and repaired the damage as best I could on my end. We are works in progress, turning inward with self-compassion, stilling the mind and breathing in and out, peace and clarity return. Be well and balanced dear one as we together heal and grow.

Lovingly,
River

Mantra for Today

May 8, 2021

What would it take to wake up the masses from the unconsciousness of greed, falseness and delusions of separateness? It feels like we are experiencing a Noah's Arc like reset. Could it be that we truly wouldn't stop consuming, doing, and using if it were not for a worldwide pandemic virus? Is now the time to react by obsessing over newsy details, speaking over one another of the latest live news stream, and be the first to rise the eye brows of the listener competing still for stage? A time where we are afraid to touch one another, to hug or show the slightest bit of affection? Should we be using the Corona Virus to distract ourselves from our broken relationships, shifting our gaze from self-accountability to join the masses in the collective panic? Or is this an opportunity? A tap on the shoulder from the Mother Ship to please take personal inventory, heal yourselves and your relationship to others and the earth?

Lovingly,
River

Mantra for Today

May 9, 2021

Regardless how traumatic childhood events were and how much grief endured; possibilities for joy and contentment exist. Everything in life offers gifts. The greater the pain, the greater the opportunity to stand powerfully resourced. As mother's day approaches tap into the divine mother earth, and the inner mother of survival. You are here, you are loved, you are worthy, you are cherished. Celebrate your birth, celebrate the mother of all life eternally giving what is needed. Today, I know I am well mothered.

Lovingly,
River

Mantra for Today

May 10, 2021

As we as a collective community on planet earth face this gift, this opportunity to stop and take stock, let's together reflect on and contribute more to ourselves and others. With less doing, shopping, eating out, socializing we now are given space to tune in. Looking within, without judgment ask yourself, How am I being? What needs my love and attention right now? Is it my body? Is it my beliefs? Is it my ways of relating? Now is a perfect time to lovingly do a personal inventory and tap on a truer self. No performance is needed right now, put the defenses aside, silence the mind and tune in with luxurious space to you! Your life matters dearest one!

Lovingly,
River

Mantra for Today

May 11, 2021

What feelings come up for you as we are asked to pause all going and doing? If you are wired, as most are, to be productive, follow a working routine, shopping and meeting people, you are likely feeling a tad antsy. It is a time to feel some discomfort while adjusting to change. What have you quietly dreamed of having a chance to pay attention to? Have you thought, if only there was more time in a day? Now, you have that extra time! A miracle! That elusive, "more time," fantasy is now yours to play with. If you are lucky enough to have your health, bask in gratitude. Maybe now you can further educate yourself, 190 Universities are offering free online credit courses through classcentral.com. List all the opportunities the Corina virus pandemic has afforded you, and smile. Your response is your freedom now.

Lovingly,
River

Mantra for Today

May 12, 2021

If you haven't yet grokked the fact that the Universe has offered you a moment to get whatever has evaded your consciousness, here is a nudge; it is time, now, dear one to heal your life. Now, in the dimension of planet earth, the earth school, you are being tapped on the shoulder, it may feel like being knocked on the head, the message is this: you must address your addictions. Address your co-dependency, address your anxiety, your belief that your value is tied up in performing. It is a gentle nudge, the Corona virus pandemic, worldwide attention and law enforced quarantine. Hey, is there anything more obvious? If you are feeling frustrated, like you got to go, somewhere anywhere but here, then that is your wake-up call. That feeling is your flashing light, calling YOU to address your habitual unconscious soul sucking, behaviors. There is nowhere out there to go for distraction, that's the point. Go within, find your balance, listen to your teachers. I am here loving you, always,

Lovingly,
River

Mantra for Today

May 13, 2021

Is your mind disturbing you? Mind vs You. Mind hungry for something wrong. Notice how when you take a bird's eye view of your current situation, there may be a sense of manageability, then comes the mind with an old narrative, something not quite right, about you! Then, comes despair. You are doing just fine, but mind convinces you are failing to thrive. It is a lie; the truth is you are having an experience completely within your realm of capability. Notice how thoughts sway emotions, energy in motion through your body, some disrupt your tranquility some guide you to stillness. Choose which story you will dwell in, you are the story, you are the narrator and you are the illustrator of the big picture. Train the mind by choosing which thought you will breathe life into. Practice mindfulness, gratitude and present time reality. You are not your past; you are magnificence in form!

Lovingly,
River

Mantra for Today

May 14, 2021

Everything is happening now exactly as it should. The world changes, sometimes gradually sometimes abruptly. Our world has seen war or earth quakes damage entire villages and cities overnight. The Covid is a gentle shift. Fear is not our friend, dear one, be gentle in your responses today. Life is good and now we can drop into the awe and wonderment of all that is. Blessings

Lovingly,
River

Mantra for Today

May 15, 2021

We have been called to isolate ourselves, refrain from our normal coming and going in the world. Some people are in fear of the future, regarding supplies and resources. Notice your thoughts, if you hold fear-based thoughts, observe your behavior. Is it calm and present? Or are you snappy and reactive? What feelings and behavior would follow if your thoughts were those of trust in a higher good for all involved? When I reflect on my past experiences, the challenging ones have taught me courage, trust and capability. Use this time of quarantine to deepen your inner strength dear precious soul, it is an opportunity to be reflective and tap in on what really matters most.

Lovingly,
River

Mantra for Today

May 16, 2021

Today is known in the Christian tradition as Palm Sunday. The day Jesus was welcomed into Jerusalem, followed by his crucifixion, followed by his resurrection. Jesus represents each of our struggles and anguish when people around us do not recognize our preciousness. We humans have a certain tendency to treat one another as though we are not cherished. We are, like Jesus was, not recognized as divine beings. When Jesus resurrected from death, he was strengthened by his suffering. The evil in the world didn't vanish, but he stood as an example of how we can overcome our hard times and gain strength from our experiences. Draw from everything available dear one, to let die what doesn't serve you, and allow rebirth; a new way of walking in your life.

Lovingly,
River

Mantra for Today

May 17, 2021

We are responsible for our own suffering. This is liberating once we realize it is our thoughts that bring suffering. Bryan Katie, in her famous approach, The Work, asks, who would you be without that thought? Taking personal accountability for our perceptions gives us power to move out of judgments, complaints and fear. Bring your focus within dear one. Notice the field of consciousness is a place where there is no right or wrong, there is pure love. Conflicts resolve from the position, "I made it mean... and that brought me suffering". An internal locus of control vs pointing at external forces is a place of true creation.

Lovingly,
River

Mantra for Today

May 18, 2021

There are those among us who are not being asked to stay home and safe. Medical personal in our communities are working tirelessly to serve the sick. Today, we park all our fear at the door and step forward each moment with gratitude for the trained professionals who will story the COVID 19 outbreak very differently than the rest of us. By pausing with good thoughts and hearts of gratitude, we support them and help them keep their energy. May you be well dear one, may you be careful, may you be at peace!

Lovingly,
River

Mantra for Today

May 19, 2021

The world is purifying itself for new life. There are mothers and fathers presently anticipating the birth of their child. This child will be born into a world that is vibrating at a gentler frequency than it was in February. Children coming in now will arrive to a world with less chemical emissions, the people are also calmer and less distracted. Now is an amazing time in history to be born, blessed with a planetary reset. When we shift our focus, we notice joy replaces fear. When we balance the losses with the gains we see all things are in alignment for our highest good. The earth has endured many pandemics, quakes, storms and tsunamis. This one is gentle, may we find gratitude in this gift, may we not waste this time in negativity focused views.

Lovingly,
River

Mantra for Today

May 20, 2021

Rise today from the dead! The death of attachments, the death of beliefs, based on traumas, of who you are. You are greater than all those identifications dear one. Today resurrected from all ideas, you can see who you truly are. Nothing "out there" can define you or harm you once you have let the ego self-die.

This day, Easter morning, live renewed. Still the mind and tap on truth, deep awareness. Nothing could be more natural. Let go of habitual ways of protecting your personal identity, and be, as a newborn innocent and curious and alert to the love that was always there awaiting your participation.

Lovingly,
River

Mantra for Today

May 21, 2021

The helmsman of a ship is constantly checking the compass as the needle sways to either side of center. Steering this way and that to keep the ship on course. Our lives are like this. We may find the results of a choice left us less than comfortable with the outcome. The waters we are navigating may be rough at times requiring greater focus and clearer maps. Correcting the course sets us right again, this is our practice. Today, just take each moment at a time doing the next right thing to keep balanced. Pause, take space, call a friend, stretch, drink water, whatever is called for to direct your compass back on track.

Lovingly,
River

Mantra for Today

May 22, 2021

Slow down, you're doing fine. You can't be everything before your time. Have compassion. Be patient with your healing soul, my love. These are important lessons that you don't want to skip over for your growth. Get inspired, creating is key to get past those unsettled feelings bubbling to the surface. You are doing beautifully as is. Today you are right where you need to be, gorgeous and free.

Lovingly,
River

Mantra for Today

May 23, 2021

The weekend begins, dimming to a close another chapter spent in the new Covid reality. You are doing well dear one. You are encouraged to accept a gift of time and space. Let the busy mind recover from its addictive demands. Ease into each new day like an unstoried song. Breath in this beautiful moment and relax. Ask your body what it likes, clear some habits that just don't serve you. No matter how many times you have stumbled, no matter how many relapses into unconscious craving, no matter how many broken promises, this new day is a clean slate. Correct and continue. Accept and change.

Lovingly,
River

Mantra for Today

May 24, 2021

When your world feels like it is falling apart and the love you seek seems to evade you, this is suffering. There is nothing more attention getting than the sting of pain, loss, and dashed hope. In times like these, spiritual practice brings us to a kind of peace we had no idea was possible. Being connected to an even higher vibrational frequency than that of met expectations and the comfort of our attachments, offers a deeper peace. Suffering has the potential to transcend us beyond our earthly dreams. Use this time of COVID isolation to still your mind, clear your heart and become familiar with your Self. You are here for a reason; the Universe loves you.

Lovingly,
River

Mantra for Today

May 25, 2021

You are living the life exactly that was meant for you. Find your true self amidst the confusion and uncertainty. Still you're doing and wanting and reaching. Today, right here, within you there is peace. No need to become, no need to do, just breath, relax and connect to the source of love within you. Remember who you are. No matter what is happening all around you, you are okay dear one. Breath and watch the trees. Peace awaits you, not in your mind, but in your true Self.

Lovingly,
River

Mantra for Today

May 26, 2021

Yesterday, I witnessed a dog killing a chicken. This happens, the instinct of a predictor overrides the human companion's ethics. When I react in indignant outrage, I activate a force within me that infuses my system with, sadness, anger, injustice, resistance and grief. It doesn't bring the chicken back to life, it only leaves me whirling in suffering. Learning from a situation and acting to prevent future events is prudent, but suffering is optional. The mind offers catastrophic judgments against self and other creating an energy field of deep discontent. We must train the mind, by shifting our focus. There was a clutch of new chicks which I now have living in my home. Where there is death, there is also birth. As I point my attention on caring for the little yellow peeps my heart expands and I am calm. I notice the conscious choice to accept what I cannot change and the courage to do what I can. Everyday there are multiple choices in the mind field to react or respond, to go spiraling down the negativity hole or climb up to the light. Perspective is the key to the gates of your own heaven. In this time of increasing restrictions from our governor due to the Corona virus, see if you can shift your attitude to gratitude and note how this feels. You have permission to enjoy what is, precious, it is the best option.

Lovingly,
River

Mantra for Today

May 27, 2021

Life is an adventure of every kind of feeling and emotion. We meet love and bask in the comfort of feeling everything is going to be okay. Shifts, changes come like the light of day that becomes the dark of a starless night. All of it experience, like the hourly dimming of the suns light, changes come. Do we hide in fear when night has fallen? Do we grasp for comfort and reassurance? Whatever is happening dear one is happening, stand strong in courage and root to the one unchanging source, the source of light within you. That light is always there, be still and contact that anchor of stable resource. You are this!

Lovingly,
River

Mantra for Today

May 28, 2021

We naturally yearn for connection with others, in particular we wish to be united with another who will love us forever no matter how our growth process affects our behavior. We are crushed when we reach for another, only to face the devastating reality that they have turned their backs to us. Although it feels catastrophic, here I offer a shift of perspective to consider. If we consider for a moment that our purpose in this life is to be solidly aligned with a higher source of love than any human form can offer, and that those who have behaved in ways that felt like rejection or abandonment are actually helping us refocus our attention on this higher source, we can shift from deflated to enriched by the apparent loss. Could it be they have acted in our highest good by their very act of unavailability? We move from needing validation from external others to filled with inner empowerment a source that is trustworthy and steady. Find the love within by refocusing your attention to stilling the mind from its obsessive grasping. You are safe here.

Lovingly,
River

Mantra for Today

May 29, 2021

There are times, like the one we are currently experiencing, where changes and uncertainty leave us in an unfamiliar place. We may not have chosen to be hurled into isolation and questionable economic futures, but here we are. If we allow the feelings and emotions stage for our observation they help us get in touch with a deeper sense that has been there for a long time. When we feel something intensely we may have an urge to push it down or numb it out. It may keep us up at night and leave us less resourced to function. This could be the dark nights of the soul. Use it for all it's worth, dear one. Follow the thread and see if you can discover what is ripe for transformation in you. Is there a belief that you don't belong? And all the performing and posturing hasn't resulted in that true embrace? Is there a grasping and clawing behavior to find your rightful place in the family of life? Having used mind altering options, physical sensations and avoiding mental, emotional and relational challenges, it all leaves you with the same gaping hole. Stillness is your bridge now to a place of self-recognition, the I who observes the life, that one is you, the rest is personality. You are home right here, at peace in your true nature beyond personality. Here, life happens where there is acceptance. You got this!

Lovingly,
River

Mantra for Today

May 30, 2021

What is presence? Have you ever been in a hoarder's space? Imagine that space before the hoarder moved in. Then there was space. Then there was pure potentiality, pure possibility. Then the stuff was moved in. Not all at once. Certain useful things, certain attractive things, certain distractive things, like a T.V was moved in. This is like the mind. Before all the distractions were piled in, fears, delusions, illusions, and doubt, there was presence. The space, before the stuff, is still there, in order to be in the space, the stuff must be moved out. Clearing the mind of distractions is presence. Each moment, mindful awareness, concentration on what is, clear seeing. Don't hoard, or obsess over thoughts that do not serve you, this only blocks your contact with what you need most. In the spacious place of presence, there is peace, creativity, comfort of being. It is simple, be still in presence. Eventually, little by little the space clears out. Maybe not all at once, but as in the stuff filled room, gradual confinement becomes gradual freedom.

Lovingly,
River

Mantra for Today

May 31, 2021

Each of us has a span of time within which to live our best lives. My dear friend, Eileen, left this life on the cusp of her 96th birthday. A woman, like you and me, with many challenges, (husband, 11 children, career, community) who despite each one, greeted life with determination and self-love. Eileen's super power was to live available. When you meet a person with radiance, you are not necessarily looking into the store window of luxury. It is not the luck you see that makes a happy person, it is resilience and ability to see past the current challenge deeper into what is more important. Eileen knew people mattered, laughter mattered, caring and feeding one another was what mattered. And as a result, her life glowed! Her death was the happiest passing. She knew it was her final hour, she called each child and blessed them with her words and laughed as her loved ones on the other side beckoned her forward, then, left her breath. Stay in connection with love and friendship dear one, everything will be alright.

Lovingly,
River

Mantra for Today

June 1, 2021

Today The word love indicates relationship with another. Loving ourselves is identifying there is the human self, having this amazing, painful, dramatic, dynamic experience every day, and the soul self who compassionately witnesses the human self. Without self-compassion, compassion towards other is more a reflection or ricochet emotion towards self. From the place of self-love, there is an expansion of love available to everyone. It may even be true that until one is in relationship with oneself, making time for oneself, paying attention to the self's needs, it is impossible to have a true relationship with another. This is what meditation is about. Breathing in and out paying attention to the subtle presence of an inner being. This is pure consciousness present in the avatar, or human body. The Covid 19 pandemic is offering humanity an opportunity to stay home, a home that no one can take away from you, a home where you are safe, that home is right here within. Check in dear one and see if you can contact that still and quiet voice loving you for all you are.

Lovingly,
River

Mantra for Today

June 2, 2021

The word love indicates relationship with another. Loving ourselves is identifying there is the human self, having this amazing, painful, dramatic, dynamic experience every day, and the soul self who compassionately witnesses the human self. Without self-compassion, compassion towards other is more a reflection or ricochet emotion towards self. From the place of self-love, there is an expansion of love available to everyone. It may even be true that until one is in relationship with oneself, making time for oneself, paying attention to the self's needs, it is impossible to have a true relationship with another. This is what meditation is about. Breathing in and out paying attention to the subtle presence of an inner being. This is pure consciousness present in the avatar, or human body. The Covid 19 pandemic is offering humanity an opportunity to stay home, a home that no one can take away from you, a home where you are safe, that home is right here within. Check in dear one and see if you can contact that still and quiet voice loving you for all you are.

Lovingly,
River

Mantra for Today

June 3, 2021

When people come together with a common cause or commitment, all differences and personal agendas disappear, and we are united. Reflecting on historical examples of this on a large scale; the civil rights movement, the equal rights movement, and many conscious commitments to make our world a more fair and kind place for all of us to live, we see the beauty of humanity. Currently we are in a worldwide pandemic crisis, calling us all to be aware of our behavior. This is good for us! It is like mindfulness is the new religion. Mindfulness can only bring more awareness of the effects of our actions. It is easy to revert to old patterns of behavior, dear one, we all tend to want what we want and want it now. See this time as an opportunity to break the unconscious drive for instant gratification and continue to be part of the community effort to heal. This healing will affect each one of us personally and spiritually as well as keep our neighbors safe. Remain with the program to end the spread of the corona virus by thinking of others before yourself when making choices.

This is our spiritual practice now. Much love,

Lovingly,
River

Mantra for Today

June 4, 2021

As spirit beings in a human aviator, we have arrived here on earth with purpose. A friend said to me yesterday that she felt she needed to be more purposed. She is kind, loving, feeds people, loves life, laughs easily and contributes without hesitation when a need arises. These are purpose enough! Since we all here have incarnated in human form, we can be assured we are magnificent beings, evolved and privileged. Instead of longing to be better people, we would do well to be mindful people. Aware of values such as kindness, health, supportive, and in tune with the heart. Viola! Better automatically! May you know yourself dear one and smile in your radiant magnificence!

Lovingly,
River

Mantra for Today

June 5, 2021

Mother's day is a significant day to pay attention to the primary role played to care and nurture others. Whether the other was birthed through our body or we mutually chose each other it is an honor to play the part. Mother /child dynamics may be intensely challenging making this marked day an invitation to disappointment. Perspective is everything, dear one. Choose to see the gift in even rejection! See the soul agreement to liberate from scripts, to awaken in you the challenge and victory of self-reliance and self-referral of your own worth. Today play with your role in mothering and in being mothered, even if not through birth mother. Choose the focus that brings light to this truth: you are a precious gift, you are lovable, evolving and valued. See love today, and turn down the invitation to focus on hurt, defy the lie and embrace the truth. With motherly love eternal,

Lovingly,
River

Mantra for Today

June 6, 2021

You have been walking on earth constantly touched by ideas of who you are. The roles you play, the family you were born into, these are not you. These are circumstances. When we get wrapped up in identifying ourselves and reactive to the things that upset us, we forget we are free. Choose to be happy, "even though and especially when", dear one. Be happy even in the disappointment, even in the uncertainty, remember who you are. How?, you ask. By paying attention to what makes you light up. What is it for you? Your animals? Your creative expression? Your service? Music? Poetry? Spiritual inspiration? Physical movement? Gardening? Certain people? Focusing on being one with your hearts joy, will reconnect you to your birth right to happiness. This life is a happily ever after life!

Lovingly,
River

Mantra for Today

June 7, 2021

Dream or nightmare? We choose through our intentions. As we are flooded with news these days, it is important to choose our daily intake, much like you do for the health of your body, (or better in some cases). It is easily forgotten that we are powerful manifesters our own reality. Are you using language of poverty or the abundance? Notice your words. Within each of our struggles is embedded is its opposite, resilience. Try this, when a fearful or devastating thought surfaces in your mind, entertain the opposite. For a few moments feel into what that would be like? For example, the thought, "I am afraid if I get sick, I won't heal", the opposite is, "I have an amazing immune system". Feel the difference. We are the creators of our own story, thoughts are rising and falling energy, observe the emotions that also rise and fall. If we react, it is charged with a sense of threat. To loosely paraphrase Henry Ford, if you think you can or think you can't, you are right. That is how powerful our minds can be. In times of uncertainty, this we can do!

Lovingly,
River

Mantra for Today

June 8, 2021

Day 90 of the Covid orders to mindfulness. It is good for us to practice awareness. To be present in taking care of ourselves and others and to be still for more of our time in our lives. There is a chance, finally, to notice with consciousness. Fears do absolutely nothing to support us. Awareness and attention in each moment, with the spirit of trust and good will, helps. Everything is unfolding exactly as it should in the natural order of things. Calm yourself from all the drama and news feeds and hype today dear one and support your nervous system with present moment awareness. Focus on the spring flowers and gentle temperatures and know life goes on.

Lovingly,
River

Mantra for Today

June 9, 2021

There is divine order in everything. As humans we spin a narrative on everything with precise positive or negative decisiveness. What if it is neither good nor bad but simply is the result of choices? Some choices result in limitations, some choices result in relationship endings, and it all is a natural occurring outcome. There is a divine order to every outcome. When we lift ourselves out of the clouds and see even though certain experiences are limiting, there are blessings of love that come rushing to accompany the journey. Be in an open field of clear space from right and wrong dear one and open up to the wonder all around.

Lovingly,
River

Mantra for Today

June 10, 2021

Each and every one of us in a body, will at some point or another experience physical hurt and limitation to a once taken for granted ability. Whether through injury, surgery, disease or slow decline, the body has a temporary quality. When one aspect is compromised through pain, suddenly awareness of the many uses the weakened part served is illuminated. We become dependent on the kind helpfulness of others. It is a good practice to humbly receive. Most of us like to be in the illusionary state of power and autonomy. Yet we are an interdependent species. Care and concern for a member of our circle expands us spiritually. Take pause today, dear one, and notice the many successful maneuvers your body parts perform each day and lovingly celebrate the usefulness of these with a certain sense of letting go. We are not our bodies; we are far greater. Everything that happens to the body is an opportunity to heal our mind and enhance our conscious awareness. There is this choreography of physicality and energy in our field; how we dance with acceptance and commitment to health makes all the difference. Where one weakens the other becomes stronger.

Lovingly,
River

Mantra for Today

June 11, 2021

Animals instinctually behave according to the medicine that made them. A dog does not doubt his tendency to bark, a cat does not feel guilty for scratching, a goat does not hesitate to eat a plant, no matter if it is someone's landscape, a chicken will happily scratch to find worms. We humans too have a natural way, but different then animals, our brains can analyze, question and conform. Beliefs lead us to behave fueled by fears of rejection, abandonment, judgment. To return to our true self, we must feel into our actions and tune into the sense of harmony with our truth or our programming. We must do this if we aim to live authentically. It may not feel appropriate at time to speak our truth, especially if another person reacts to it, but in the bigger sense, we must be true to ourselves to feel alive in our species. Check in today, see how you feel as you interact. This is not easy since programming is brain washing. There is a thought that rings, "put up and shut up", conform, be agreeable, go along with it all. Don't you owe it to yourself to now and forever more move in your life from a place of truth?

Lovingly,
River

Mantra for Today

June 12, 2021

To be Compassionate and tenderhearted towards those who hurt us is less likely if we cannot first generously practice these qualities to ourselves. There is rarely a human that has not experienced some sort of rejection, judgment or ill treatment in their lives. These experiences, if not addressed through compassion and tender care, can drive deep into the psyche leaving the person feeling flawed. You are not flawed, there is not something inherently wrong with you, dear one; you may have unattended wounds that still to this day leave a residual effect. Turn inwards with tenderness, feel where in the body these emotions reside and bring to those hurts understanding and love. We do not see people as they are, we see people as we are. Until we heal ourselves, we cannot truly see other. Feel my embrace.

Lovingly,
River

Mantra for Today

June 13, 2021

Even when something happens that is not your preference, peace is still possible. We can react with great resistance to what is, or we can calmly witness with inner equanimity. There are things we do not have control over. Whether, at one time, a relationship was the pivotal center of our universe, and then something unforeseen changes the connection, through death, or betrayal that beloved no longer engages in ways that we once enjoyed, still there is peace. True peace is not reliant on outside occurrences dear one. Find your center, remain connected to your own true source, and from there watch the coming and going of the dance of relationship. My loving support is with you always,

Lovingly,
River

Mantra for Today

June 14, 2021

Each person and situation we encounter, offers us growth. If a person is critical and hurtful, if we feel rejected and hurt, we can learn how criticism harms. This learning, though painful, holds the potential to practice kindness to others. Let us not repeat the cruel treatments visited upon us but let us transform that behavior by doing better towards others. Martin Luther King preached, "Hate begets hate; violence begets violence; toughness begets a greater toughness. We must meet the forces of hate with the power of love". (1958) We do not have to be robotic mirrors of the hurt we have experienced. Not only do we change the world by doing the opposite, but we heal ourselves as well. When we can heal ourselves of the hurt we have experienced, we can truly show loving kindness to a world so in need of this. Much love and compassion always,

Lovingly,
River

Mantra for Today

June 15, 2021

Mother Teresa stated to the world, We "forgotten that we belong to each other." In May 2020 a climate of violence has erupted inevitably as injustice and inequality has been reaching a boiling point now for centuries. "Otherness" and "ingroup" mentality divides people causing suspicions towards the unfamiliar. For true evolution to take place, we must find within ourselves a trust in the common qualities in each human, shared. No one is an outsider! Each one of us belongs to one another. In a world of divorce and break ups and fractured families we mistakenly see others as disposable. Rather, realize, each person is a significant helper on our path to evolution, especially those whom we do not recognize as like us. We learn not from sameness, but from the reflections identified as unseen, untapped aspects within us, in another. Those who behave in ways that challenge us, see through the lens of compassion, for self and the human mirror before us. This world will change when in our own small area, we shift our mentality to clear seeing, a brother and sister in all we meet. You belong dear one, trust this!

Lovingly,
River

Mantra for Today

June 16, 2021

There are a few real gems, or keys of wisdom that make all the difference as we face change, uncertainty and that which we have no power to influence. Acceptance and Adaptability. We can only truly accept, once we first allow our feelings, thoughts and emotions expression. The trick is not to act on them but to at least release them. Without full exploration, repression masquerades as acceptance. Make no mistake, repression may appear like contentment, but woe is he who overlooks this distinction. Repression manifests as disfunction eventually. Adaptability comes following acceptance based on conscious expression of all facets of the situation until you find peace with it. If the situation involves a relationship dynamic which makes no space for expression, express through art, writing, or speaking to a trusted listener. What is your deepest desire? Under all the fear of uncertainty, under the disappointment, under the angst, what true wish for yourself lays there?

Lovingly,
River

Mantra for Today

June 17, 2021

Throughout history inequality has caused suffering to women, people whose skin is not white, the uneducated, and the poor. There is a hierarchy visible and invisible setting the standards of whose voice is listened to and who is ignored. We are capable of correcting this injustice by first recognizing the subtle ways we discount those near us. The hurts unheard, the needs unmet drive a deep root of harm into the individual which ultimately affects the whole of humanity. Begin by making space available for conversation. Nonviolent listening means listening without being defensive, listening for the intent of what is being expressed, listening with compassion. When pain is first expressed it may not be eloquent or scripted in perfect prose, so listening without judgment is essential for healing. There is hope for a Just world, it begins with you and me dear friends.

Lovingly,
River

Mantra for Today

June 18, 2021

Amidst the changes happening all around us right now, there is a silent change within us. We are affected by the occurrences of our world, if we open ourselves to embrace everything as a catalyst for the greatest good for all involved, we lean into change with a willingness. Yes, some of the things happening seem catastrophic, people are targeted by police because of the color of their skin. This is unjust, and it has come as a result of silent racism covertly operating in our system. This had to come to a head! We have to unite and wake up to the collective oneness of all beings regardless of race, economic status, gender identity, religion and so on. We need the catastrophic to cause change. What epic changes do you now address that have your attention? What possibly silently waits at the border of acceptance? The change within you, meeting your true self, is your invaluable gem, with this wealth, you are resourced to influence a greater outcome than what might have been imagined.

Lovingly,
River

Mantra for Today

June 19, 2021

A personal narrative is a powerful script that places squarely before the mind's eye a lens through which the world is seen and believed. It is important to question the story we tell ourselves. Stories can be locked doors behind which we live, thinking we are safe. So common is it to hear a person describe their life in review, as hard. This story not only describes the life history, but also sets the stage for the next episode of "hard life". It is not exactly natural to question the mind but know that all descriptions are like little locks securing windows as well as doors around you. What would it be like to, with blanket statement, declare, "my life is growth, expansion, change, wonderful, a story of resilience"! Think if all the ways you label yourself and ask, is this freeing me or locking me up?

Lovingly,
River

Mantra for Today

June 20, 2021

Some of the qualities of the father are leadership, fair and reasonable goal setting, integrity (keeping promises) and protection. These characteristics are wonderful when present in the father figure In a family. It is important to know that each of us has a father part within to guide and protect our life path. Whether a father man showed this example or was incapable for whatever reason; these qualities can be accessed and lived from conscious cultivating these aspects within ourselves. Today I will celebrate Father's day by channeling father qualities.

Lovingly,
River

Mantra for Today

June 21, 2021

Loosen the grip. Recognize today what you cling to. Identity, skin color, physical appearance, sexual orientation, status, grievances, patterns, roles, beliefs, opinions, knowledge, all of it tightly gripped, all ideas of personal self. Who am I without these? Unbound. Let go of all these ideas for a time, is there peace? When it is recognized, the grip loosens and there is space. Liberation from personal identity allows true nature, presence.

Lovingly,
River

Mantra for Today

June 22, 2021

When we experience struggle there is an opportunity to adjust our goals, plans and behaviors. We learn in the struggle that something needs attention. Is it thought habits? Is it attitude? Are its old beliefs that be Mantra for Today When we experience struggle there is an opportunity to adjust our goals, plans and behaviors? We learn in the struggle that something needs attention. Is it thought habits? Is it attitude? Are its old beliefs that behoove us? Is it relationship patterns in which we lose yourself? These are the gifts of struggle. When we are comforted, we risk going back to sleep. We risk rocking back into our rut. So, use the struggle, milk it for all it's worth. The gems harvested serve to make us rich in important ways.

Lovingly,
River

Mantra for Today

June 23, 2021

When we experience struggle there is an opportunity to adjust our goals, plans and behaviors. We learn in the struggle that something needs attention. Is it thought habits? Is it attitude? Are its old beliefs that behoove us? Is it relationship patterns in which we lose yourself? These are the gifts of struggle. When we are comforted, we risk going back to sleep. We risk rocking back into our rut. So, use the struggle, milk it for all it's worth. The gems harvested serve to make us rich in important ways.

Lovingly,
River

Mantra for Today

June 24, 2021

In his extensive research and study, author, Bessel van der Kolk, offers great insight into physical manifestations of emotional stress in his book, The Body Keeps the Score: Brain, Mind, and Body in the Healing of Trauma. We are not our bodies, and we are intimately connected to the vessel we move in on earth. Chinese medicine has known this connection for 4 thousand years. Our difficulties or un-addressed struggles in life are neatly tucked away in our bodies, lying dormant until eventual activation, and present in the form of disease, or as we therapist term, dis-ease. This is inspiration to face the suppressed self-defeating thoughts and ideas, or conclusions made in early childhood and so forth, before they present as a physical problem. The body is a friend in the expression of the block, by bringing awareness. Pause and explore the message and begin to deal from the inside out. My loving support always,

Lovingly,
River

Mantra for Today

June 25, 2021

Love is core. When a child is harshly reprimanded, the wound of rejection takes root. Like a seed lays dormant in the dark, if it is watered with shame, abandonment and hurt, it grows and becomes an identity. Anger may surface as a defense against more insult and injury but at the root is the suffering of that primal wound. Dig down into the soil in which this seed of identity is planted and pull up these false messages dear precious one. Remember who you are, born to an earth that feeds you, supports you, surrounded by spirits who cherish you and love you. If the initial messages have confused you and caused you to forget, find the voice of kindness inside yourself and compassionately care for your life force. This life is yours, therefore distance yourself from harshness and love yourself as you so deserve.

Lovingly,
River

Mantra for Today

June 26, 2021

To be companion with an animal is like being assisted by angels. As we endlessly crave excitement, lost in distraction, they patiently stand by. Happy to see us, ready to ground us, as we offer them pats; they seem to sense we need it as much as they do. The fireworks were too much for my wee dachshund, so he ran 2 miles uphill in the middle of the night. I searched all night, remembering how I got annoyed at his barking. I'd do anything to hear him bark now, I thought. Mercifully, he was safe. The moment of clarity was this; to appreciate now the gifts of this life, for this too shall one day pass.

Lovingly,
River

Mantra for Today

June 27, 2021

One precious life. Born to the circumstances of our birth. Our first responsibility is to be in our lives. Were we controlled by adults? Were we steeped in religious limitations? Was the society of the time racist? Sexists? Homophobic? Unjustly righteous? How do we move through all that to a more balanced existence? Practice. It doesn't matter what the practice is, if it is meditation, or prayer, daily inspiringly reading, a walk-in nature, but some practice that rights you on your authentic path. Start with changing the language used to describe yourself and your life and step INTO a more genuine expression of your one life.

Lovingly,
River

Mantra for Today

June 28, 2021

It might be said that it is impossible to be in relationship with other without conscious awareness of your true self. Conscious awareness is being strongly rooted in presence as witness of one's own personality. To know conscious, "I" is witnessing personality. Lost in identification with personality makes impossible relating with other. Personality is defending ego, personality casts others in roles. Personality has stories of me. The realization that I am not all my titles and acts of this stage called life, frees me to love all regardless of how they present or behave. Observe the personality from the perception of the "I" witness or true self. Here there is no judgment, no fear, no ego, no status, no stories. Be aware of true self.

Lovingly,
River

Mantra for Today

June 29, 2021

Ross Rosenburg wrote, The Human Magnet Syndrome: Why We Love People That Hurt Us. The premise of this work is that Love Respect and Caring are expressed on a continuum in a relationship based on the individual's capacity to offer these. Some couples are polar opposites, one giving more at the cost of their own needs, one giving less and benefiting from the outpouring from the other. He states there are self-oriented and other oriented personality types. When a couple's pattern is such where they operate at opposite ends of this scale, the imbalance perpetuates the longevity of the relationship despite the unhappiness it causes. This is the basis of habitual relationship dynamics. There is hope for recovery. Awareness of the dynamic at play is key, self-compassion and boundaries support shifting these automatic systems inviting more balance of Love Respect and Caring into your life.

Lovingly,
River

Mantra for Today

June 30, 2021

If it is truth we want, then everything serves to realize truth. Fears are loaded with illusions. An idea of limitations invites fears to control us. We become slave to fear, reducing ourselves in our mind. We declare to ourselves and others, "I am not capable". Once we challenge these fears, with "what if?", "then what?", and expose what lurks beneath the subconscious we find truth. If we are consciously available to truth, truth is revealed through every experience, so long as we do not close our eyes to what is unveiled, we can see. Truth and trust come together, there is then nothing to fear.

Lovingly,
River

Mantra for Today

July 1, 2021

"Out beyond ideas of wrongdoing
and right doing there is a field.
I'll meet you there.
When the soul lies down in that grass
the world is too full to talk about."

-Rumi

Our communication with others is too filled with opinion, judgment and disagreement. What would it be like to meet in the space of neutrality and simply bear witness? Ego wants to be right. To divide into camps of sameness. Too easily we toss people into categories according to our point of view. Trust me dear one, our views are limited, some don't see beyond their own navels! Be in beginners mind today and see what wants to happen. Trust in your own foundation, there is nothing to fear, there is no threat. Lay in the expansive space of nature and simply empty yourself of thoughts, opinions and labels and experience freedom.

Lovingly,
River

Mantra for Today

July 2, 2021

It is important to watch how we story who we are. If we tell ourselves and others that who we are is reflected on our losses, we invite more of the same. If a relationship has ended, we may say, I was a bad judge of character. This brings in doubt when new love walks towards you. A certain skepticism floods the pure space of possibility. Once you get through the hurt and anger that loss has left, you start to remember the beautiful aspects, and if you are committed to growth, you see the hard times as gifts. Growth is our trajectory. Do not be scarred by deceit, betrayal and disappointment. If you cannot let go, let be. Everything is a lesson. When the hurt resurfaces, Just notice without story, this is a natural experience, memories can leave us unstable. Smile upon yourself dear one, you have loved without filters, everyone you have invited in has been an angel. Love with beginners' heart, knowing that based on all the previous experiences, you are now more resourced to choose wisely.

Lovingly,
River

Mantra for Today

July 3, 2021

You are not your mind. The mind is like an annoying roommate who is riddled with fear. It doesn't always present as fear, but presents as resentment, anger, suffering, annoyance, but at the core is fear. The mind suggests, you are not safe, you are reliant on the approval of others, if they harm you then you are doomed. It is not true dear one! The truth is in the present moment you are safe. Your security is in knowing your true self. In observing that mind is tempting to drag you, your true self, out of the present moment, out of freedom and into bondage. People will validate the fear-based mind, this becomes very convincing that others are villains. The truth is, those who have harmed you, are also imprisoned by their fear-based mind. Get some distance from your mind and be in a place of oneness with all of life. Your freedom waits for you as you unbind yourself from the enmeshed state with the illusionary mind. When the mind plagues you with thoughts, stop the thoughts and inject the opposite. If it says, you are unloved, inject, I am deeply loved, I love this life I live, and that inner love radiates and attracts true love from all who see me. Your mission today is to train the mind. It is a tool not your master.

Lovingly,
River

Mantra for Today

July 4, 2021

On the fourth of July people pull out the stops and celebrate. Fireworks are bought with abandon. Peaceful evenings are blasted with flashes of fire and booming explosion. To many this type of celebration is exciting and wonderful. To many others, including animals and some of those who've experienced war, the sky filled bang bomb and clap eruption is terrifying. It is like this with trauma. Fear replaces calm, a rewiring of the nervous system causes reaction. The goal is to see things as they are. Is this a real threat? Or is this person just making loud noises? Today I practice being a calming presence for myself and others no matter what environmentally I cannot control. Becoming a solid source of inner security (sovereignty) I resource myself in my safe place, my inner sanctuary.

Lovingly,
River

Mantra for Today

July 5, 2021

It is in the dark that the seed sprouts! Life on earth is one difficulty after another. Rare is the one who was raised by stable and conscious adults. Most people have abandonment issues sistered with rejection issues. Loss of relationships, loved ones, health, and youth is on everyone's syllabus here at the earth school. The constellation is growth. We learn to appreciate, we learn how our unconscious behavior patterns impact us, we become stronger through the dark times much more so than when we think we have it all under control. The universe loves you and knows your trajectory is evolution. Recall that through ever difficult period, you were supported and assisted. You are on track, dear one, accept each challenge as a gift, something is changing there is a deepening and expanding when we take a broader view.

Lovingly,
River

Mantra for Today

July 6, 2021

As we are all now clearly aware that the planet has come to its very edge of accommodation for greed and careless self-satisfying humans, we can no longer afford to ignore our responsibilities and the need for right action. It is time to simplify, to create a new way of being here. We need less manufacturing of plastic, less fuel use, less wastefulness. Can we look together to a new world where we take care of ourselves and others in consideration for our mother home? Life has called us to pause, what seems in front right now is healing the wounds of our earth and in that we are sustained and homed. Destruction followed by reconstruction, the order of things.

Lovingly,
River

Mantra for Today

July 7, 2021

Inspiration from Rob Brezny
It's always the beginning of the world.
Even if you don't call yourself an artist, you have the potential to be a
dynamic creator who is always hatching new plans, coming up with fresh
ideas, and shifting your approach to everything you do as you adjust to
life's ceaseless invitation to change.
It's to this part of you -- the restless, inventive spirit -- that I address
the following: Unleash yourself! Don't be satisfied with the world the way
it is; don't sit back passively and blankly complain about the dead weight
of the mediocre status quo.
Instead, call on your curiosity and charisma and expressiveness and lust
for life as you tinker with and rebuild everything you see so that it's in
greater harmony with the laws of love and more hospitable to your soul's
code.

-Lovingly River

Mantra for Today

July 8, 2021

The word apocalypse has been heard in social circles and media broadcasts to describe the state of the world right now. There are fires, a global pandemic, hurricanes, riots, racial conflicts, political battles and earth quakes, (not to mention the usual isms at play on any given stage). Reactions to the upheaval are fueled by the collective narrative as shared fear of uncertainty is common. The threat response in the brain doesn't know the difference between reality and story. What we say and agree with affects our nervous system causing heightened levels of stress hormones. "What is" does not need to be met with negativity and panic. Animals live in the moment and react when necessary; humans have the unfortunate ability to perceive imaginary outcomes as catastrophes. We also have the fortunate ability to calm our minds, choose our language and support ourselves and others in challenging times. We are not in control of the what is, but we are in control of our contribution to our own state and have an influence on how others address the current situations. Today: Act where necessary rather than react to the unknown, refuse negative language, focus on gratitude and spread love. The world and all sentient beings need our support right now.

Lovingly,
River

Mantra for Today

July 9, 2021

The word apocalypse has been heard in social circles and media broadcasts to describe the state of the world right now. There are fires, a global pandemic, hurricanes, riots, racial conflicts, political battles and earth quakes, (not to mention the usual isms at play on any given stage). Reactions to the upheaval are fueled by the collective narrative as shared fear of uncertainty is common. The threat response in the brain doesn't know the difference between reality and story. What we say and agree with affects our nervous system causing heightened levels of stress hormones. "What is" does not need to be met with negativity and panic. Animals live in the moment and react when necessary; humans have the unfortunate ability to perceive imaginary outcomes as catastrophes. We also have the fortunate ability to calm our minds, choose our language and support ourselves and others in challenging times. We are not in control of the what is, but we are in control of our contribution to our own state and have an influence on how others address the current situations. Today: Act where necessary rather than react to the unknown, refuse negative language, focus on gratitude and spread love. The world and all sentient beings need our support right now.

Lovingly,
River

Mantra for Today

July 10, 2021

Justice Minister Ruth Baden Ginsburg is remembered this week as a stand for equality for women, minorities, people of various complexions at the highest level of American law.

Justice RBG lays at the US Capitol, the first woman and Jewish person in history to do so there. As a society, progress towards equality has been slow and there are threats of things going in reverse! We are in an age where global travel affords us greater opportunity to learn about the world's religions and customs. There is no excuse for ignorance and ethnocentrism. If we as individuals refuse to silently permit divisive slurs, open our hearts and minds and dialogue with even those different from us and be a stand for fairness for all beings, yes the fur and feathered as well, we together create a world to live joyously in for all of us. Let us continue what one tiny woman effortfully launched forward. Today, with curiosity (not judgment) listen to understand. Be committed to contributing to the highest good for ALL.

Lovingly,
River

Mantra for Today

July 11, 2021

Relationships change. Once we were a part of, then apart. Once we invested energy, then we feel obsolete and redundant. The mind says, rejected; maybe more accurate to say excluded. Yes, there is loss, yes it hurts, yet to make it personal drives the experience into shame. If actions and behaviors contributed to the dynamic shift, own your part, if possible, make amends. Then take care of yourself with self forgiveness, self compassion and let go with love. Relationships change. Learn from them and lovingly move on. The experience was rich, bitterness has no value, regret serves no purpose; acceptance, forgiveness and compassion lay the path before you.

Lovingly,
River

Mantra for Today

July 12, 2021

"The mind can pursue sensations, desires, but it cannot pursue love. Love must come to the mind. And, when once love is there, it has no division as sensuous and divine: it is love. That is the extraordinary thing about love: it is the only quality that brings a total comprehension of the whole of existence."

- Jiddu Krishnamurti

True love is boundless and universal, it's a state of being which doesn't discriminate between white and black, us and them, or even you & I. In many ways, love is a state of being, the very essence of life, because it's the energy we feel when we come in contact with things in a very deep and authentic way. Our true nature is that of an interwoven tapestry, both interconnected with all living and non-living beings and interdependent upon so many various conditions it would be unwise to say we exist independently, separate from the rest of existence. The love we feel when we look deeply into ourselves and the world around us, both realize and directly experience the deep connection we share, is the way to fully realizing our true interconnected nature and realizing our inherent "wholeness".

Lovingly,
River

Mantra for Today

July 12, 2021

I am you and you are me. It is false to think anything is happening to you; what is happening, is happening for us. We are not separate, humanity, animals and birds and insects, all inter connect. What is expressed through one, vibrationally impacts all living beings. It is a false belief to think you are alone. Your hurt is my hurt, your joy is mine; we are reflections always. When you need love, give love, when you have a windfall, share. Loving others is loving yourself. Today, see in others yourself, tune in to what is needed in you and receive it through giving.

Lovingly,
River

Mantra for Today

July 13, 2021

All suffering comes from the mind. There is such a thing as sickness without suffering. I have personally enjoyed the company of individuals going through health challenges with joy and happiness. It is when we fuse our ideas of ourselves, and images of identity with certain states, such as health, that we are susceptible to suffering. We are far greater than our health, far greater than our addictions, far greater than our behaviors. All of these are results of thoughts and beliefs. We are not guilty of thoughts, we are not to blame for our state. We simply forgot who we truly are. My teacher, Mooji, encourages us to use "mind attacks", as opportunity to see where we are still attached to an identity of self. Remembering who you are brings a neutral witness to all states without suffering or judgment. From this loving place we can change. My loving support is with you!

Lovingly,
River

Mantra for Today

July 14, 2021

The year of 20/20 hindsight has been an invitation to reflect, pause and reorganize. Mystics and wisdom seekers and lovers of truth have risen to the occasion to bring voice and perspectives to help people around the world embrace the amazing opportunity in what might otherwise be seen as pure chaos. To access a fresh and inspiring new view on this past year and what is to come, I offer you:

"The Power of Love: Resetting Humanity to a New Way of Living on the Earth" Global Oneness.

Humanitystream.org

And, "A Magnificent New Normal"

Magnificentnewnirmal.com/event

Richard Rohr in his daily: Center for Action and Contemplation states:

"... with steady practice it will eventually give us the ability to stay present to what is, and meet it with wisdom, compassion, and courage".

Consider dear one that no matter the challenge you currently face, there is a silver lining. Everything is happening for you to transcend out of ignorance and into an expanded awareness of your true nature. Today, I am grateful for everything! The joy and heart break, the hurt and the help; it all is orchestrated for the highest good, for ALL involved.

Lovingly,
River

Mantra for Today

July 15, 2021

Our true nature is stillness,
The Source from which we come.
The deep listening of pure contemplation
Is the path to stillness.
All words disappear into It,
And all creation awakens to the delight of
Just Being.
—Thomas Keating, "Stillness"

We humans are meaning makers; we story every experience most often as "good or bad", (over simplifying here). Teachers like Keating, Bryan Katie and Mooji guide us to being present to what is happening without the mind stirring up emotions and narrating conclusions. Being still within while responding to true crisis allows a steady stable response in the face of chaos. Today, be in agreement with reality, not resisting the pain, the traffic, the construction, the dogs barking, the relationship break up. Loving life and reality with equanimity while also taking action to change what you can.

Lovingly,
River

Mantra for Today

July 16, 2021

Your presence here on earth is a sign of your magnificence. You have been born to both challenge and opportunity. The challenge offers growth. Who would you be without the lessons from struggle? We learn from loss, we learn from disappointment, we grow to see that loss helps us be conscious of the value of our relationships. Through disappointment we learn to adjust our goals and dreams and be discerning. Opportunity is there just beyond the threshold waiting for us to open to newness. Expand your view and see beyond the petty and step forward to greater possibilities. Whatever you now deal with will pass. Patiently watch, change will come. Your life is a series of magical moments.

Lovingly,
River

Mantra for Today

July 17, 2021

As Americans pensively await the results of the 2020 presidential election, the following thought comes to mind. Humans, along with all life forces, at the core are non-violent. When healthy, we seek to move peacefully. When out of balance, greed and fear possess and a "power over" replaces fair engagements. We have daily models of this on our public forums offering the wrongful impression that "might is right", and the strong armed "man" wins. Think of a world where collaboration and intention for equal good for all involved is our possibility. Today, I move in my small circle with fairness, gratitude, respect, and kindness. In this way I see a greater potential for the larger world in people and all other life forces.

Lovingly,
River

Mantra for Today

July 18, 2021

Love is the life breathed into each and every living being. I am bold to say it is what all of us seek beneath all our actions; even when those actions seem oppositional to easy access to love. We are taught in order to be loved we need to be good. So, we behave in ways that suppress our authentic feelings and needs. This is self-betrayal. Love in the healthiest natural form comes unconditionally; we are cherished and considered. When we realize we must stop betraying ourselves by allowing others to treat us without regard, we enter into the possibility of realized love. Richard Rohr offers us this, "To only love ourselves is escapism, loving only our opponents is self-loathing, loving only others is ineffectual". I would add, begin loving yourself by forgiving all the ways you have been mis guided and forgiving others will follow; thus, true love made possible.

Lovingly,
River

Mantra for Today

July 19, 2021

Love is the life breathed into each and every living being. I am bold to say it is what all of us seek beneath all our actions; even when those actions seem oppositional to easy access to love. We are taught in order to be loved we need to be good. So, we behave in ways that suppress our authentic feelings and needs. This is self-betrayal. Love is the healthiest natural form comes unconditionally; we are cherished and considered. When we realize we must stop betraying ourselves by allowing others to treat us without regard, we enter into the possibility of realized love. Richard Rohr offers us this, "To only love ourselves is escapism, loving only our opponents is self-loathing, loving only others is ineffectual". I would add, begin loving yourself by forgiving all the ways you have been misguided and forgiving others will follow; thus, true love made possible.

Lovingly,
River

Mantra for Today

July 20, 2021

Things are not always as we think they are. Hurt feelings stem from being triggered. Something happened a longtime ago that left us feeling disposable, unimportant, unsupported or outside the group or family. Now, in adulthood a word or action or situation trips the switch, or trigger, and the same feelings flare up as though true. Remember this dear one, it is feeling strong so that you can recognize it and sever the tie to the original inflicted pain. As a grown up, you have more resources to deal with hurt feelings. Pause now and get some space around the hurt, feeling change. Act only from a calm resourced place.

Mantra for Today

July 21, 2021

The main task towards adulthood is to being self-aware. Life's bumps and bruises, insults and injury can leave a person reactive. Blaming others for how we feel only keeps us stuck. At times, it is easy to feel victimized when misunderstood we react, rebuke, defend and attack back. None of these reactions feel like choices but they are. On some level the mind is committed to a certain view. Thoughts lead to feeling which lead to actions and reactions. This is the basic tenet of Cognitive Behavioral Therapy, CBT. Once the emotions settle down, take the time to expand the thought process and see what else is true. Sometimes getting space from what is stimulating the thoughts is helpful. Meditation and prayer can take you to higher ground where a calmer mind offers new insights. Be aware beloved one, life is not trying to harm you.

Lovingly,
River

Mantra for Today

July 22, 2021

Dog companions enhance every mental and physical health. No other friend is as devoted to knowing me as intently as my dog. I am accepted exactly as I am; hair disheveled, shirt inside out, makeup or not, I am adored by my canine pal. Everything is better with the dog by my side. It is an undeserved blessing while on planet earth to share the journey with a devoted dog friend. Today, I am honored to keep good companionship with my loyal friend and live to meet my doggies ideal of me.

Lovingly,
River

Mantra for Today

July 23, 2021

To enjoy good mental health is something to be truly grateful for. It is good to acknowledge what contributes to wellbeing and to give credit to all of our helpers. Four legged, furry, feathered, scaled and shelled beings as well as the bipeds in human form all have rich gifts to offer on any given day. Remaining calm, like the still pond or stable like the high mountain are invitations to embody nature's secrets to balance and harmony. Today I lift my spirits in gratitude for the helpers and guides all around me. If I am quiet for a moment of undistracted focus, the guidance and love rushes in to support. We are not alone.

Lovingly,
River

Mantra for Today

July 24, 2021

The Green Sea Turtle in the Pacific Ocean around the island of Maui is known by the Hawaiian word, Honu. Locals revere this beautiful ancient being as a family member. The honu is on the endanger species list, therefore the locals take personal responsibility to protect the honu's safety, space and privacy. As humans we are enriched by the chance to swim with and observe these beauties in nature. The turtle symbolizes spiritual teachings in first nations tribes such as the 13 moons, a celestial symbol of motherhood. Mother earth, or turtle island, carries humankind on her back. Today, I am in awe and wonder with deep respect for all of Mother Earth's creatures and the helpers they are in my life.

Lovingly,
River

Mantra for Today

July 25, 2021

There is a cycle in everything. The season comes to an end allowing the birth of the next season to take its place. Where there is death, of old beliefs, identification with ego, stories, self-harming behaviors there is birth. New possibilities, greater wisdom and cultivated ways of being. The former self was exactly right for the time, and as in all things, a dynamic change is immanent. With deep relevance for the sacredness of life move forward dear one. The gifts called in are surrender and gratitude.

Lovingly,
River

Mantra for Today

July 26, 2021

Unresolved childhood trauma can result in false perceptions of self and other. Fearful experiences can cause us to be protective and defensive even though the current environment is nothing but safe. It is a worthy journey to work with a professional therapist to address the past. The goal of therapy would be to integrate the events of childhood with new adult understanding. We are not cursed to live our whole lives imprinted with the actions of unskillful caregivers. Being resilient, we move through the painful abandonment and skillfully navigate new situations even when they trigger us. Today I give myself the gift of beginning to heal.

Lovingly,
River

Mantra for Today

July 27, 2021

There are going to be "nay say-ers", on your path, whose own world view is negative and fearful. These people can be very convincing in their talk of how drastic your choices are and the dreadful conclusions that will surely come. Feel into your own heart space and gut. Take a moment to check in with your own higher wisdom. It will take courage to disagree at times, but this action is an investment in self- confidence. A beginning of self-referral leads you to do what is in your personal highest good. You got this!

Lovingly,
River

Mantra for Today

July 28, 2021

When an important relationship seems to be in peril, think of it as an opportunity. Relationships can become robotic and sleepy. We humans like predictability yet, this can land us in a rut. When things begin to feel like the rug is being pulled from underneath you, it may be time for an expansion. Take some time alone dear one, and refrain from making any conclusive decisions. Allow your partner space as well. Time apart for a brief time, receding council from those who know and love you may prove to be what is needed to shake things up and see what lands. Old NJ patterns may be obstacles to true closeness and authenticity. Embrace the changes that pain is offering. Thinking this as a birth not a death.

Lovingly,
River

Mantra for Today

July 29, 2021

Author, Toko-Pa Turner, in her book, Belonging, states: (paraphrased) Ghosting someone is an act of indifference. Like making yourself a ghost in your own life; it counters belonging. As if you don't believe you've made an impact, you become disassociated from the importance of your presence. Deeply rooted in the belief that other people (and yourself) are disposable. Until we take accountability and hold others accountable; we can never take a seat at the table of belonging. Most of us prefer to avoid conflict. Research has shown that humans predict a far worse experience than what actually happens when a situation is directly addressed. Being accountable is about owning your part. Speaking truthfully without judgment and blame can lead to closer deeper relationships. Today I will do an internal inventory of who I am ghosting emotionally or physically and truthfully address what is blocking me from speaking my truth.

Lovingly,
River

Mantra for Today

July 30, 2021

Until we can forgive our mothers we will always harbor self-rejection. There is a direct link between self-sabotage and long held resentments of our mothers. They birthed us, we came from them, and even though we may have legitimate grievances against them until we set ourselves free of long held grudges we will forever be yoked to self-hatred, felt inferiority manifested in behaviors that behoove us. Our mothers are humans and like us were mistreated, misunderstood and acting from the skill base their lives afforded them. Today I will list my grievances against my mother and one by one apply understanding and compassion with the intention of liberation.

Lovingly,
River

Mantra for Today

July 31, 2021

Self inquiry is a practice of true seeing what runs unconsciously in our automatic patterns. Looking without judgment at our qualities; which have been reactions to the world around us. A spiritual practice begins with self love. Love for self and acceptance of all aspects, with a willingness to choose which thoughts, feelings and behaviors create a more peaceful existence. Negative thoughts will come, unmet needs breed judgment. When we become self response able, we speak truthfully about our feelings and needs removing blame from the equation. Freedom is the perfume of self accountability. I observe my human tendencies without identifying with them. I choose to love myself and others forgiving both when unconscious behaviors result in hurt.

Lovingly,
River

Mantra for Today

August 1, 2021

Our bodies are listening! It is truly amazing how impressionable we are; our mental and physical aspects are taking direction from the thoughts we have. Some people do not realize that we can direct negative thoughts to tune the volume down by turning up the more adaptive inspiring thoughts. I choose healthy food because I prefer it to junk food. I am strong and healthy, my body loves me. My animal's bodies are my priority, I feed them natural food supplemented with essential minerals and vitamins. I love and respect elders and patiently honor their needs and I learn from their wisdom. I will be loved and cared for when I am an elder. I appreciate the service offered in stores and essential care professionals. Every one is working together in my world.

Lovingly,
River

Mantra for Today

August 2, 2021

The thinking mind offers a cacophony of distracting, fearful and negative thoughts. We collapse the past with an imagined future and the present escapes us completely. We humans possess the power to choose; when it occurs to us to steer the mind in the direction of our highest good. Life loves you! Happiness and peace is FOR YOU! Begin this day with a commitment to change the mind's narrative to a more uplifting one. I am willing to change. I accept myself and I am forgiven. I am becoming free as I choose thoughts that support me. I am the friend I need in another. I am the loving partner I seek in my partner. I am surrounded by opportunity and welcome new experiences.

Lovingly,
River

Mantra for Today

August 3, 2021

In the uncertainty of the world we now live, we must learn a way to be comfortable. Resistance and demanding things be our way points to a need for security. Security comes from an inner stability in the changing circumstances of the external environment. Living mindfully means being present in each moment. Acceptance and Commitment Therapy, (ACT) teaches to notice what is thought or felt and choose thoughts and actions that are based on values to reach goals. This is a conscious practice when committed to brings that secure feeling each needs in the precarious world we live. We don't need to know everything, we can't know everything, with a mindful practice, however, we can be comfortable with the unknown. Living peacefully rather than in anxiety is a worthy goal. Today I will choose thoughts and actions that bring peace.

Lovingly,
River

Mantra for Today

August 4, 2021

Relationships are the sweetness and spice of life. When in harmony, there is appreciation, acceptance, attention, affection, attunement and allowance for individuality. When any one of these qualities are missing the balance is off and the flavor turns bitter. It is important to be responsible for the energy you bring into the sacred beloved container. Are you available? Can you tune into your partner? We have the power to create the gentle journey we need the most. Conscious coupling is a skill and an art. Today I will be present to my contributions.

Lovingly,
River

Mantra for Today

August 5, 2021

As we edge towards solstice, December 21, the planets Jupiter and Saturn will be closer together than they have been since the Middle Ages. In the sky it will look like 1 planet! Astrologists say this is a good time to make decisions. It feels safe to say that 2020 has been a year of sever challenges for everyone alive on planet earth. We are wise to reflect with gratitude for the learning opportunities inherent in struggle. I have learned to let go of old patterns of expectations. Expecting restaurants to serve me, expecting to be allowed to freely meet and move to my personal preference. Expecting people to stay the same as they once were in a dynamic we together created. For me, 2020 has offered me the gift of letting go. Letting go is the bottle within which is the perfume of trust. I trust in life, love, the natural world to re-organize, the ability of people to make new and better agreements with one another based in a greater personal truth. Live by your values and create your vision for 2021. How you will straighten up from the bends of the past and fly right towards the bright star of possibility? Blessings to you, dear ones, and thank you for sharing this year with me!!

Lovingly,
River

Mantra for Today

August 6, 2021

Personal identity is the first attachment bondage. With the holiday of Christmas just barely behind us, many of us have spent time with our first human family. When you were born, you were given a name, a birth order and right from the beginning you have been defined and described. Are your families descriptions of you who you are? As I have moved forward into my own adult life I became certain roles, yet these titles are not who I am at my core. I have been on a seekers journey to discover who I am, I took a spiritual name to allow space between my assigned persona to experience authentic self. Identity is limitation. When consciousness is brought in and a willingness to let go of all definitions or projections is present, the emptiness of name, role performances, and descriptions of character are left behind, there is contact with soul self. The word "Being", is a clue for our self realization, I ask myself am I being still? Am I being Love? Am I being True? This gets me in contact with who I am spared of external labels assigned by opinions or subjective experiences. Celebrate awakening with awareness that all the identities assigned are not who you are. Who you are is deeply pure. Discover the truth of who you are beyond identity.

Lovingly,
River

Mantra for Today

August 7, 2021

One of the things that blocks our experience of a full expansion post relationship is the dualistic mind. Humans have to be taught that we can simultaneously love someone and move towards different goals. Too often when relationships end there is so much resentment and judgment that love gets buried beneath the cloak of hurt and loss. When we take full accountability for our own experience; our thoughts feelings and versions of reality, we can resolve them without blame and shame on ourselves and our former partner. This is unconditional love. When love and loss are held in balance we can behave towards our endings with honor, respect and gratitude. We treat ourselves and the one we no longer share a couple hood with as a spiritual agreement which served each in the highest good for all involved.

Lovingly,
River

Mantra for Today

August 8, 2021

When you think of the many roles you have played in your life, you notice they change. When a child, you played the role of one to follow parental directions. You were student, a role involving assignments, tasks and responsibilities that you now no longer do. You may be mother now or father or teacher or some other title; yet these too change. When you sit in stillness, imagine these cast personas as actors on the every changing episodes of your personal show. Who are you beneath or above all of that? What about you have you noticed does not change? If each role was a cloak, and was removed, what is at the core? We can get lost in roles and titles and attached to a script. What happens when that becomes out dated? Loss? Or freedom? It really depends on your conscious practice of true seeing. If we play our roles with a willingness to fully contribute without clinging to it as if it defines us, we shift with ease and grace. If there is space for the dynamic changing of things there is no fear. In improve class I learned how to jump into new and unexpected stories letting go of the previous. Not to say what was didn't matter, it was magnificent in its moment; and, now and now and now something new. We may say we are not getting older, we are becoming new. My love is for you, beloved friend.

Lovingly,
River

Mantra for Today

August 9, 2021

We all have negative thoughts. It is somehow in our wiring. Back in the day we had to do what we could to survive. We had to make sure we didn't get kicked out of the tribe, so we worried what other's thought of us. Excommunication meant death. Oddly, centuries later we still have that propensity to worry. The trick is to develop a committed effort to override the fear response. Today I will bring my psyche up to date, I will practice turning within for my approval.

Lovingly,
River

Mantra for Today

August 11, 2021

Complaints seem to be tethered to some belief, some thought that a situation should be other than it is, or a person should be different than how they are. Complaints seem to be masquerading as truth. When I expand my understanding, I see how my complaint limits me. When the light goes on and an insight presents, greater understanding replaces the old complaint and there's acceptance. Today, I will examine my complaints and explore where I am defended. Where some fear or narrow belief is causing complaints. Mantra for Today : Complaints seem to be tethered to some belief, some thought that a situation should be other than it is, or a person should be different than how they are. Complaints seem to be masquerading as truth. When I expand my understanding, I see how my complaint limits me. When the light goes on and an insight presents, greater understanding replaces the old complaint and there's acceptance. Today, I will examine my complaints and explore where I am defended. Where some fear or narrow belief is causing complaints.

Lovingly,
River

Mantra for Today

August 12, 2021

Loving another sometimes means taking difficult actions. It is so easy to prolong our suffering by enabling a loved one as they make promises to be better (in the future). The irony is as long as their action have no real consequences, making those hard changes falls to the back burner. Tough love is, well, tough! Today I create boundaries by saying no to chaos and yes to change. As I take care of myself, I trust another person's ability to do their self-care. In the present moment there is the real world gazing straight into our eyes. Addressing what is here now is like taking one step, one moment at a time. Catastrophic thinking is like walking into a dark theater, a horror movie of oncoming unknown fears. The "what ifs" of life VS the "What is". Today I choose what is in front of me and remain in my movie.

Lovingly,
River

Mantra for Today

August 13, 2021

There is a comfort in knowing what to expect. We like to walk into a known place, and have it look as we've known it to. A grocery store has food organized according to categories, churches have pews and a preacher, Certainty is preferred over uncertainty. This however becomes problematic when a certain belief based on a previous experience becomes the expected when encountering new situations. As a child becomes accustomed to criticism, when people are encouraging there is discomfort; "this was not expected, this is unfamiliar, it doesn't fit into what is already known". Some people will become suspicious, discount the encouragement and translate it into criticism, because that is what was known and familiar. Today, I will practice shifting from the comfort zone of certainty and stretch into new realities. I will challenge my already knowing and invite new possibilities. Mantra for Today : Complaints seem to be tethered to some belief, some thought that a situation should be other than it is, or a person should be different than how they are. Complaints seem to be masquerading as truth. When I expand my understanding, I see how my complaint limits me. When the light goes on and an insight presents, greater understanding replaces the old complaint and there's acceptance. Today, I will examine my complaints and explore where I am defended. Where some fear or narrow belief is causing complaints.

Lovingly,
River

Mantra for Today

August 14, 2021

What would it be like to wake up to a new day without a single negative thought? No yesterday's problems, no regrets, no held resentments? What would it be like to see each person without previous disappointments and decided character flaws? Today, just for fun, I'm going to practice present moment spaciousness. As I breath slowly in and out, I am innocent of negativity. I am free.

Lovingly,
River

Mantra for Today

August 15, 2021

Thank you! This morning I woke up. All of yesterday is past, what lays before me are moments of opportunities. I get another chance! I can repair what needs repairing, I can correct and continue, I can create new possibilities with every word and action. Holding onto grudges is a burden. Today I can choose to carry or put down. I will decide to do what is best for me and all involved.

Lovingly,
River

Mantra for Today

August 16, 2021

It is important to pause and take notice where I channel my life force. Our energy is like a tank of gas, if we aren't conscious, we allow it to leak out. Focusing on what other people think of us, is a leak of energy, people pleasing and morphing ourselves into being something in order to avoid or control an outcome is a huge spill of energy. This leaves only fumes to move in the direction of our values and goals. Today, I will do what fills my tank, and be with people in ways that gives my life energy. Only I can live my life. I will stop spinning around spilling energy "in order to..." I will live in choice.

Lovingly,
River

Mantra for Today

August 17, 2021

Religion as a pure practice (before power and control spoiled its appeal) was a practice of "respect for what is sacred, conscientiousness, sense of right, moral obligation and divine service". Humans that have shunned any spiritual practice; seem to struggle to deal with conflict by attacking and blaming themselves and others. A "practice" can be a 12 step program, a recovery refuge, stillness, self-accountability; humbly admitting responsibility for behaviors and attitudes, and a commitment to right thoughts, right actions and right livelihood. We all need direction on this map of human life. Today I will see where my life needs managing, take moral inventory, and choose a practice to live more responsibly. If I have conflict, I will first look at myself.

Lovingly,
River

Mantra for Today

August 18, 2021

When shame is no longer a default setting, I can humbly look at my own actions and admit where I have been un-skillful. It's okay to be human. It's understandable when we error, even repeatedly; and, it is our responsibility to do better. Relationships are built on each person contributing in ways that keep the relationship healthy. Today I will, apologize when wrong and forgive when wronged.

Lovingly,
River

Mantra for Today

August 19, 2021

Communication is a highly complex delivery and exchange tool conveying ideas, plans, changes, and feelings. When used skillfully, understanding and co-creation is a wonderful outcome. There are times, more often than not, when the communication intent misses to land successfully. Feelings are hurt and stories begin to swirl in the imagination. Today, I will be clear with words, and when something lands in me as offensive, I will ask for clarification.

Lovingly,
River

Mantra for Today

August 20, 2021

Knowing my boundaries allows me to clearly choose what I am committed to participate in and how much I am responsible for. When a relationship isn't equally invested in, when one person wants it more than the other, there's an imbalance of give and take. Negotiating change with two adults means each is in choice. Each looks at their own behavior and honestly considers if they are contributing to keeping the relationship healthy. Blaming, accusing or pleading creates a dynamic of friction Willingness, accountability and a vision of what is preferred creates connection and mutual respect. Today I will respond according to my boundaries of self-respect.

Lovingly,
River

Mantra for Today

August 21, 2021

Belonging is a powerful need. Little children learn how to curb their enthusiasm, tone down their voices and to act and look in order to belong. So much originality is sacrificed through this conditioning, this exiling parts of our true essence. We become actors in our own families, so convinced of our performance we lose ourselves. Today, I will begin reclaiming myself by addressing the feeling of disconnect. I am on a journey back to myself; my home.

Lovingly,
River

Mantra for Today

August 22, 2021

When I use negative words to describe myself, I betray the most important friendship in my life. Being friendly to myself supports my earthly experience. Betrayal of self creates an insecure environment where I don't belong and am not supported. Life is what I make it by lovingly guiding myself every step of the way with compassion, forgiveness and words of encouragement. Today I will begin using only words of love and kindness to describe myself.

Lovingly,
River

Mantra for Today

August 23, 2021

We humans share a great deal in common. We all know what physical injury feels like, we know emotional pain and suffering, we all know craving and desire. However, the degree to which we feel, our coping strategies, our emotional intelligence, and frequency varies from person to person. At times one may unconsciously project their internal angst onto another. This is a violation of boundaries. Knowing what is mine and what is projected from another's energy field allows conscious boundaries. Today, I will tend to my humanness and refrain from projecting unconsciously.

Lovingly,
River

Mantra for Today

August 24, 2021

Hurt people hurt people. Each of us have reacted from our wounded selves. In those moments we are not bad, we are in pain. What is called for is an inner perception shift from judgmental to compassionate. Compassion is defined as a "keen awareness of the suffering coupled with a desire to see it relieved." When another is hurting us, it may be necessary to leave the relationship. Still, compassion over judging and blaming sees the pain as the cause. A compassionate response is not trying to change or fix that person, it is simply empathy.

Lovingly,
River

Mantra for Today

August 25, 2021

Pain is inevitable, suffering an option. Suffering is a state of resistance of what is. We don't want this turn of events we have pain in the body and say this should not be happening. This refusal to accept creates a mind field of suffering. Depression and anxiety are products of mental versions of what is happening. We say no. This is wrong. I don't want this, I want what I don't have, this is suffering. To be free of suffering practice acceptance. Acceptance doesn't mean I agree or endorse this, but it is what is. In this now reality there may be pain, but suffering is far worse and that can be mitigated by the practice of acceptance.

Lovingly,
River

Mantra for Today

August 26, 2021

We are born worthy. The journey between those potent moments of birth and death is infused with opportunities to question our validity. Breath is all the proof needed to ensure value of life. There are a multitude of opportunities to learn through trial and error; each one a rich opening for growth. As we go along, we develop certain qualities that we can adopt that make the journey harder or easier. One such quality is attitude. The mind can be trained to optimism or succumb to curmudgeonly. Every experience in life is a lesson supporting our birth right to realize our potential today. Today I choose so see the growth opportunities and embrace my worthiness to a good life.

Lovingly,
River

Mantra for Today

August 27, 2021

You attract into your life whatever you think about. Your dominant thoughts will manifest. Pay attention to your emotions. Think about your desires. Don't think about what you don't want. When you notice yourself feeling bad, you've caught yourself thinking about something you don't want. Turn your focus back towards what you do want, and your emotional state will improve rapidly. Be the director of your thoughts. As you do this repeatedly, you'll begin to see your physical reality shift too, first in subtle ways and then in bigger leaps.

Lovingly,
River

Mantra for Today

August 28, 2021

Don't take it personal. When we are solid in ourselves there is a strong foundation. Knowing we are imperfect we are open to feedback. Our imperfection is not tied to our worth; we are students in life. From this position of self-assurance we can look at ourselves and admit where we are stuck in old beliefs and interfering behaviors. We can be playful with insights another may offer. We can open to broader self-knowledge. Taking things person leads to defensiveness and creates additional conflict losing the gift offered. Today I will commit to loving myself and be open to consider feedback.

Lovingly,
River

Mantra for Today

August 29, 2021

When reflecting on the past there may be moments where we cringe. Humiliation shadows the whole screen, no redeeming qualities are seen. It is imperative that we understand that we are all works in process. Mistakes are expected, inspected, accepted and corrected. We are not the same as we were, those humiliating moments taught us; in fact, they were helpful to assist our growth. Today, I embrace who I am including my embarrassing past.

Lovingly,
River

Mantra for Today

August 30, 2021

Toxic thoughts take hold of reality and taint an otherwise innocent moment. Addressing habitual thinking patterns one by one takes conscious effort. Actively reaching out for a preferred way of being in the world is a practice. The tendency to worry is replaced with new thought; "life is unfolding for the highest good for all involved". The fearful thought, "What if I disappoint others?" is replaced with, "I am generous where I can be, other people's reactions are not my business". Today I will actively reach towards reframing toxic thoughts with helpful thoughts; using the language of what I am becoming instead of what I don't want to be.

Lovingly,
River

Mantra for Today

August 31, 2021

The mind is a meaning making machine; it will assign an interpretation of any innocent event. An untrained mind produces anxiety. In order to live a life of peace and contentment it is essential to train the mind. Notice which thoughts bring distress and notice which thoughts bring ease and choose the latter. The mind can be trained and in training it you create the life you wish to live; it makes all the difference! Today I will practice mindfulness and choose thoughts that support me. I will stick to the facts. I will notice which thoughts are assumptions. I am willing to change.

Lovingly,
River

Mantra for Today

September 1, 2021

There is a saying, "Trust in God but tie up your camel". Similarly, the serenity prayer, "Grant me the serenity to accept the things I cannot change, the courage to change the things I can and the wisdom to know the difference". Both instruct us to be responsible and to surrender. There are desperate people who, from their pain, rob trusting people. There is a lesson in this. To remain conscious of the many ways we are privileged and to take responsible action to prevent crime. Privilege comes with responsibly. Take nothing for granted. The thief was once an innocent child; life's traumas shaped their world view to be that of desperation and unmet need. Today I am deeply aware of the choices I have been privileged to choose. Not everyone is so fortunate. Practicing compassion and locking my doors prevents participation in unhealthy dynamics.

Lovingly,
River

Mantra for Today

September 2, 2021

As the seasons change feelings of loss naturally come. The Human being cycles through seasons much like all of the natural world. If we cling to a time or experience with a sense of, this is as good as it gets, fear creeps in through the drapes of the next stage. If we reflect, we observe that each stage, each phase has brought a mixture of joy, beauty, happiness and grief, loss and struggle. Notice too, dear one, you handled it all! Be in the place of openness, I like to say, I belong to the church of what wants to happen, this, or something better.

Lovingly,
River

Mantra for Today

September 3, 2021

When an animal is traumatized it reacts defensively. It is possible to misread it as aggressive and dangerous. Fear arises and we want to push it away and withhold our affection. If we are patient and can see beyond the trauma reaction the animal relaxes and begins to trust; there is sweetness there beneath the fear. It is like this with humans as well. At the core, there is a deep seated need for love in all beings. Today I will see beyond another's defensiveness based on their fear reaction and give my love. Love heals.

Lovingly,
River

Mantra for Today

September 4, 2021

Good morning. As this new day blinks open its sleepy eyes, I am becoming aware of the rich possibilities before me to make choices that support me. Every moment is bright with options. As I reflect on behaviors that have not supported me in my past, I see they have been impulsive. I can learn to pause and respond, choosing what comes out of my mouth choosing what goes into my mouth. This will be my practice. I live today by clear intentions.

Lovingly,
River

Mantra for Today

September 5, 2021

We as a species of humans have the unique ability to change the lens through which we see any circumstances. This is our power tool. By changing our views, we literally shift from one vibrational frequency to another. Even the darkest perspective, when turned around can bring light in. Childhood is over, examine the effect it has had, see where you have patterns of reaction based on not feeling loved enough, and after fully feeling the hurt, anger, sadness and grief, see if you can let it go and move into a greater spacious experience. Healing is your sole responsibility, your parents were flawed, as are all humans, don't hold them at gun point for the rest of your life. Self-sabotage is when we, on some level, stay damaged in order to punish our parents. Blame only keeps us stuck forever feeling like the victim. You are bigger than you once were, forgive the past, have compassion for those who you see as perpetrators and learn to live released from the burdens of anger, hatred and hurt. You are better than your rage, you are bigger than your past, you are the sole creator of your reality, I believe in your magnificence. My heart is with you,

Lovingly,
River

Mantra for Today

September 6, 2021

Toko-Pa Turner, in her book, Belonging, states: (paraphrased) Ghosting someone is an act of indifference. Like making yourself a ghost in your own life; it counters belonging. As if you don't believe you've made an impact, you become disassociated from the importance of your presence. Deeply rooted in the belief that other people (and yourself) are disposable. Until we take accountability and hold others accountable; we can never take a seat at the table of belonging. Most of us prefer to avoid conflict. Research has shown that humans predict a far worse experience than what actually happens when a situation is directly addressed. Being accountable is about owning your part. Speaking truthfully without judgment and blame can lead to closer deeper relationships. Today I will do an internal inventory of who I am ghosting emotionally or physically and truthfully address what is blocking me from speaking my truth.

Lovingly,
River

Mantra for Today

September 7, 2021

What would it be like to wake up to a new day without a single negative thought? No yesterday's problems, no regrets, no held resentments? What would it be like to see each person without previous disappointments and decided character flaws? Today, just for fun, I'm going to practice present moment spaciousness. As I breath slowly in and out, I am innocent of negativity. I am free.

Lovingly,
River

Mantra for Today

September 8, 2021

Thank you! This morning I woke up. All of yesterday is past, what lays before me are moments of opportunities. I get another chance! I can repair what needs repairing, I can correct and continue, I can create new possibilities with every word and action. Holding onto grudges is a burden. Today I can choose to carry or put down. I will decide to do what is best for me and all involved.

Lovingly,
River

Mantra for Today

September 9, 2021

It is important to pause and take notice where I channel my life force. Our energy is like a tank of gas, if we aren't conscious, we allow it to leak out. Focusing on what other people think of us, is a leak of energy, people pleasing and morphing ourselves into being something in order to avoid or control an outcome is a huge spill of energy. This leaves only fumes to move in the direction of our values and goals. Today, I will do what fills my tank, and be with people in ways that gives my life energy. Only I can live my life. I will stop spinning around spilling energy "in order to..." I will live in choice.

Lovingly,
River

Mantra for Today

September 10, 2021

Until we can forgive our mothers, we will always harbor self-rejection. There is a direct link between self-sabotage and long held resentments of our mothers. They birthed us, we came from them, and even though we may have legitimate grievances against them until we set ourselves free of long held grudges we will forever be yoked to self-hatred, felt inferiority manifested in behaviors that behoove us. Our mothers are humans and like us were mistreated, misunderstood and acting from the skill base their lives afforded them. Today I will list my grievances against my mother and one by one apply understanding and compassion with the intention of liberation.

Lovingly,
River

Mantra for Today

September, 2021

Today is like a newborn, fresh, innocent and new. Whatever no longer serves me, I shed, that which is possible, I invite. Long held resentments are toxic and blacken my view. Today is about redemption and moving forward in a good way.

Lovingly,
River

Mantra for Today

September 11, 2021

Being a human means experiencing uncomfortable feelings and being reactive at times. I give myself permission to feel what I feel and when tears come, I allow that. By becoming my own best friend I am not alone and I no longer criticize myself. Self-care means, self-understanding and self-validation. Like the AA tradition offers the acronym H. A. L. T, when I am Hungry Angry Lonely or Tired, I give myself a break and know that it's time for self-care.

Lovingly,
River

Mantra for Today

September 12, 2021

There is freedom in truth. When there is truly a "Yes", when agreements are made, there is full presence. When the agreement is made out of obligation, there is distraction. Excuses and reasons, even physical symptoms, block full participation; the heart and soul are in turmoil. When we have the courage to speak our truth, clearly and kindly we are spacious. True relationship with self requires truth; only from there is authenticity possible.

Lovingly,
River

Mantra for Today

September 13, 2021

We all want to be seen in a good light. We want others to be generous with us by giving the benfit of the doubt; assuming our good intentions. That doesn't always happen, people jump to conclusions based on fears. It helps if we can see what is happening and remain calm. Reacting only brings drama, conflict and unnecessary emotional upheaval. Today, I will practice breathing slowly when accused, pause, and empathize until the other person feels heard enough to allow understanding. I will relax knowing my side of the street is clean.

Lovingly,
River

Mantra for Today

September 14, 2021

Change happens. We are in New situations each day. We have learned from past hurts enough to know the difference between situations that have similar features but are not the exact same. Each new person we meet has the potential friend within them. Today I choose healthy friends and trust myself. Inner trust is my go-to. Do I have boundaries? am I resilient? Am I accountable? Do I refrain from Gossip? Do I have integrity? Am I non-judgmental? And am I generous have ready to let go of the little things? Do I allow myself forgiveness when I am at slightly off course? This builds trust.

Lovingly,
River

Mantra for Today

September 15, 2021

This new day is a clean canvas onto which I create. Who I will be in this days expression is 100% my making. Will I be who I've been? Or will I step up and be my possibility? Today I choose to be at ease, to move consciously and to pause before I speak slowly and clearly. I am love. I love my life and it shows in how I treat people around me. My boundaries prevent unconscious tangles with others. Life is my masterpiece.

Lovingly,
River

Mantra for Today

September 16, 2021

Becoming conscious of the origin of a "quirk" in self-image, is called shadow work. Following the tread, beginning with a destructive behavior (the symptom), to a false belief adopted (or thought of as true) at an early age, can lead to insights. Once the light is shone on these original self concepts, the shadow no longer has the power. This is the goal of therapy. Today I will be aware of destructive thoughts and actions and see if I can identify a decision I made about myself or the world and challenge that belief with the question: Is this true? I trust that embracing truth, I will no longer be ruled by shadow beliefs.

Lovingly,
River

Mantra for Today

September 17, 2021

I was sitting on a bench with a beautiful soul at the dog park yesterday and she said; God consciousness wanted to know itself so divided from the one to the many, (us). To truly know oneself is to love the being one is. This is not to say, to love oneself one needs to be perfect. No! It's to love the human we are. The human experience of sensations, suffering, grief, happiness, defects, quirks, warts and all! Today I will love myself and all the other ones, who like me, are parts of the whole God consciousness.

Lovingly,
River

Mantra for Today

September 18, 2021

The body is like a chariot we have the privilege to travel around our worlds in. It carries our emotional baggage neatly tucked until we are ready to lighten the load along the way. Our journey through life: developing self-esteem, creatively expressing our uniqueness, acting according to our will, loving, speaking, knowing and connection to source are all energies, (known as chakra). The balanced chakra system is like soaring along in this magnificent chariot on smooth road. Today, I will care for my chariot, my body, mind and spirit.

Lovingly,
River

Mantra for Today

September 19, 2021

As we work on correcting false ideas of who we are, we grow more self-assured and the things that once triggered us no longer have a charge. We begin to see we are uniquely gifted. We are masterful where we thought we were weak. Life is not a journey of making it all easy, life is a journey of being skillful at handling the challenges. No one outside of ourselves needs to change, but we change how we feel, how we react, and what we make it mean. Today I acknowledge my growth.

Lovingly,
River

Mantra for Today

September 20, 2021

As students of this Earth School, we need to take breaks from our hard lessons. We need to stop the studying and get our heads out of the books and take a breather. Yesterday the search and rescue was disassembled after the long intense anquishing search. Celebrations are in order. Everyone can breath gratitude. We are all better for the experience. We are closer, safer, more loving. We see the oneness of humanity because of the hard time. This is what being a student of life is like. Today I remember to take it easy. To be grateful for all the help. The suffering has an end. I re-member.

Lovingly,
River

Mantra for Today

September 21, 2021

So many sensations are felt in the body. Long held emotional traumas, feeling (both positive and negative) physical tightness, movement, temperature. When I stop and simply be with the sensations; I allow spaciousness. My inner world has more space more room to observe from the witness standpoint, more ease. As I practice self-love I wake each day and say, I love you, what do you need. A friendly voice gentles the human journey, and it is mine.

Lovingly,
River

Mantra for Today

September 22, 2021

When we are small children, traditional folklore feels comfortable. We are told what to do, how to behave, and what to believe. Then, the very thing that brought comfort, brings inner conflict. What we took for undisputable truth, no longer makes sense. We begin to think for ourselves. We begin to ask, "is this true for me"? There is a gap, a mini crisis as we transition from unconscious following and conscious decision based on direct experience. Today, I will affirm myself and befriend my inner wisdom.

Lovingly,
River

Mantra for Today

September 23, 2021

There comes a time when the long held habits, addictions and defense patterns must be dropped. The jealousy no longer leads to attention, the eating disorder no longer supports the belief that thin equals love, the alcoholism no longer brings a buffer to reality. It's time to unlock the self imposed prison gate and step up. Today I become who I'm meant to be. Free and responsible.

Lovingly,
River

Mantra for Today

September 24, 2021

Each morning I wake with this thought, "Good morning beautiful, thank you for waking up, I love you, today is going to be amazing". As a human the mind body relationship, like any relationship, is dually influenced. One effects the other. Thoughts of fear, doubt, doom bring body contract, tighten, heart rate increase. Thoughts of acceptance, ease, and optimism bring comfort, well-being and calm. I get to choose! Today, and everyday, I choose thoughts that support my human experience.

Lovingly,
River

Mantra for Today

September 25, 2021

We attract our teachers into our lives. Teachers are people who we see as having some quality or have developed some skill we notice would make a difference in our lives. Friends are often these teachers. The confidence one exudes, the ease one moves through difficulties, how another applies gentle humor, all examples to follow. That which attracts us, lives in us; maybe dormant, but there nonetheless, waiting for an invitation to express itself through our thoughts and actions. Today I will see my teachers and pay attention.

Lovingly,
River

Mantra for Today

September 26, 2021

It is deeply painful to be misunderstood by those closest to us. When we are triggered and reactive, this is but a snapshot of who we are. If our beloveds then speak to others, presenting a series of snapshots as evidence of our personhood, it feels like betrayal. The trust is broken, and the relationship is in crisis. These are painful times. Today I will trust the universe is unfolding for the highest good for all involved. Sometimes what feels like a catastrophe is a push towards something far better.

Lovingly,
River

Mantra for Today

September 27, 2021

Life asks of us this, attention. When the myriad of distractions divide us, we give a little of ourselves to a lot of things. Eventually we are on auto pilot and unconsciously go through the motions. Relationship bonds begin to weaken, symptoms of ill health start to creep in, emotional imbalance become the norm. By beginning to be single focused (mindful) life starts to show its mysteries; things begin to feel better as everything is seen and felt rather than skimmed over and passed by. Today I will practice attending to my moment by moment experience.

Lovingly,
River

Mantra for Today

September 28, 2021

Life is a magical journey of discovery. We live many lives in a single life time. The trick is to be flexible. Who I am today is not who I was at 5 or 15 or any other marked phase by a number. Circumstances are changing and so am I. Today I will adapt to life as it presents an opportunity to step across new thresholds.

Lovingly,
River

Mantra for Today

September 29, 2021

Personal transformation can precede a phase of discomfort as the previous rituals and norms begin to fade away. This is a time when helpers and guides come rushing to assist for a higher vibration is being called in. Knowing the shifting stage will present challenges we drop into the discomfort by asking, what is birthing in me? What new and purposeful way of being is life asking me to step up to? Today, I will honor my spirit and retreat into silence so that I might hear the call.

Lovingly,
River

Mantra for Today

September 30, 2021

We are given many opportunities to practice accepting what we cannot change. When confronted with negativity, boundaries help. Boundaries can be expressing truth, or imaginary protection, (like a bubble around the energy field) to prevent toxic energy from affecting us. Knowing when to express and when that would not be safe is using wisdom. Today, I will remind myself to practice self-care, and remember this is temporary.

Lovingly,
River

Mantra for Today

October 1, 2021

Facing one's humanity can be sobering. When it is no longer possible to deny imperfection, when the stark naked truth of a patterned behavior has been revealed as recklessness; whether as driving over the speed limit, texting while driving, the lack of conscious care in relationships with others, or laziness with details, it can be hard to face. Shame and guilt won't help, although a natural reaction. Self-compassion and mindfulness will help. Today I will become more committed to doing my best. I will address my reckless behavior and make amends to those my behavior has affected.

Lovingly,
River

Mantra for Today

October 2, 2021

By addressing my traumas from the past I begin to change. As I become clearer minded and begin behaving like a full-grown adult, I practice non judgment. Today, I focus on supporting my own growth by becoming comfortable with the uncomfortable feelings. Recovery may feel like pushing the rock up hill, but eventually it rolls down the other side. I will never give up.

Lovingly,
River

Mantra for Today

October 3, 2021

Imagine what life would be like without criticism. If self-approval, self-understanding, self-acceptance trumped the voice of the inner critic. Imagine today with head held high, shoulders back and a smile that says, "yeah I know I'm not perfect, but I'm good enough". Today I will choose to focus on supporting my life with loving what I am.

Lovingly,
River

Mantra for Today

October 4, 2021

St. Francis of Assisi was an example of a spiritual influence who knew all of nature is family. Humans who have decided trees are for furniture, land is for our purposes without compassionate consideration for the life in it have missed the point. In Hawaiian the phrase, Malama the Aina, means care for the land. It is a principle upheld and revered seeing plant life as members of our tribe, or we of theirs. As spring shows promise of new growth, see this as a mirror within as inspiration of proof that everything has potential for true expression. Today, I invite you to see through a new lens; we all are creation, if you feel so does all life. Tend lovingly to yourself and all other people, trees, plants, animals, feathered and buzzing. Channel St. Francis and you'll be in harmony.

Lovingly,
River

Mantra for Today

October 5, 2021

An untamed mind is a force to recon with. It is confused, bringing with it feelings like an unhandled pressured hose. This AND that, 2 minds (or more) colliding with opposing thoughts all at the same time. Decisions made that have colossal effects on others, then, doubt re-enters and the roller coaster ride starts again. Today I will commit to practicing mindfulness and doing my inner work; my life, and those around me, deserve peace.

Lovingly,
River

Mantra for Today

October 6, 2021

This day, I am faced with a blank canvas. Yesterday, and time in memorial is behind me. All my stories of who I am, all my fixed ideas of my family and how they see me, all the hurt, past. Before me now is possibility. Like an artist with a palette of fresh paint, how I choose to be in my life will design my creation. Today, I will affirm my life with supportive self-talk, assume nothing, stay curious and respond with loving kindness.

Lovingly,
River

Mantra for Today

October 7, 2021

Uncomfortable feeling point to long held assumptions that are believed to be true. Feeling unsafe points to an expectation that someone or something outside of myself is responsible for my security. This may have been true when I was a child but now my security is my responsibility. I am safe through my choices. I feel according to my perceptions. Am I collapsing my past experiences of betrayal onto current relationships? Am I assuming the people in my life will hurt me like those people in the past did? Today, I will see with beginner's eyes. See new situations without casting the shadows of past hurts upon them.

Lovingly,
River

Mantra for Today

October 8, 2021

Yesterday, I was given an opportunity to care for an abandoned, premature, hours old kitten. With optimism, everything was done to improve the chances that this wee life would thrive. There are forces beyond human control that dictate life and death. Today, I bask in the privilege of all interactions, even those that end in grief. Every opportunity is a gift of engagement. Every exchange a teacher. A basic Buddhist teaching is to take refuge in the Buddha, the Sangha, and the Dharma. The Dalai Lama added, "and when that doesn't work, I take refuge in my good intentions". What would my life be like if I let go of doubt? If I embraced my humanity, letting go of an idea of who I should be. Being who I am, with my fumbling attempts, with my errors, with this body, all of it with radical acceptance. Today I practice unconditional friendship with my life. And most important to trust my good intentions.

Lovingly,
River

Mantra for Today

October 9, 2021

Being human involves receiving instruction from sources intimately personal to each individual. Sources such as the body, mind, and intuition. When out of balance with self, mind becomes an unreliable source, body is ignored and intuition inaccessible. When in balance, the mind is in its rightful place, as a tool for thinking and planning. The mind cannot be a trusted master. It may offer, "you are broken, messed up and hopeless". Today I will find my balance by feeding my system inspirational guidance. I will listen to my higher self (intuition) and do the next right thing for my life. When somebody important to me suddenly stopped speaking to me, 6 months ago, and appeared again yesterday as if nothing happened, I had to resist the urge to confront, I wanted them to know how hurtful that was, and demand answers, explanations and an apology (and in my fantasy hear some empathy of what that must have been like for me). Instead, I choose to be who I am when not hurt. Confident, loving, curious. Living without expectations and agendas isn't easy, but it does have better results. Today I will honor my feelings and once the other person is ready, will be willing and open for clarity. People are complicated, understanding the layers of reactions take stability and wisdom.

Lovingly,
River

Mantra for Today

October 10, 2021

What does it mean to be taken advantage of? It is to allow another to take advantage of the generosity offered. And allow someone to serve and support you in the way they feel willing to. Receive the love, open up to the flow of unrestricted goodness that is directed towards you. Today, I will remind myself, I am worthy, I can take advantage, in a good way, of everything that is available to me. When I allow myself to be still, I experience space. The constricted feelings loosens, there is an expansion where before there was choking fears, pressures, worries and committed grievances. As I sit I find my way back to my inner home. Here I easily see choices. Whatever causes tightness can be let go. Whatever brings light can be enjoyed, embraced, brought closer as I practice stillness.

Lovingly,
River

Mantra for Today

October 11, 2021

When things fall apart and I notice I am trying desperately to keep it all together I need to pause and pay attention. Maybe power greater than myself is trying to reach me. Maybe my old patterns, my previous coping strategies are no longer working. Today, when the urge to find relief from an external source arises, I will turn inward. My inner guidance calls for stillness in the chaos. As they say in Hawaii, try wait. I am human. It is important to identify which thoughts are helpful and which do not serve me. I can't exactly get rid of negative thoughts and feelings but, I can challenge them by asking, "is this true"? Today I will invite thoughts that support my happiness and acknowledge I also have negativity.

Lovingly,
River

Mantra for Today

October 12, 2021

Even though relationships involve dynamics between people, I still contribute to my own peace and happiness by managing my internal reactions. I did not cause the other's patterns; I cannot control nor cure anyone other than myself. Today I practice strategies to maintain my inner state of wise mind. When a hurtful event happened in childhood I wasn't able to respond to it so I stuffed it. Now when somebody in my environment does something similar I'm triggered. Unconsciously I project my initial reaction on to the current person it's not that they are not behaving similar to the original offender, but they are not the original offender. Today I will feel my feelings and see if I can discharge that energy that was installed a long long time ago by pausing and not reacting to the current situation, this is using rational mind.

Lovingly,
River

Mantra for Today

October 13, 2021

Each moment in nature reminds me of being in the present moment, grounded. This is a moment of pure blessings. Mother nature holds me in her beautiful embrace. From this place I am open to clear seeing. Love heals all. Learning personal accountability is choosing freedom. There is no pleasure from giving into the urge to blame, the emotional outburst only becomes worse once unleashed. Trust is broken and the relationship is damaged. Today I will feel my feelings without assigning blame; this is not easy, but the outcome of peace and freedom is worth the practice.

Lovingly,
River

Mantra for Today

October 14, 2021

To be in a healthy relationship it is important to distinguish between willingness and willfulness. When one partner makes a suggestion, willingness has a tone of cheerfulness and the response of, "sure, I can do that". Willfulness has a tone of resistance with an answer of reasons and excuses. Willfulness begins a crack in the foundation of friendliness. Today I will be open to participate in my relationship willingly. If I keep bringing up the past, it'll never be the past, we all have regrettable moments, times we are not proud of. Self-loathing is like repeatedly punishing ourselves and giving ourselves no possibility for a clean start. Today I will make the next moment better by acknowledging the hurt I feel and forgiving myself in order to move forward.

Lovingly,
River

Mantra for Today

October 15, 2021

I am growing into who I was designed to be. I've made sacrifices, I've experimented, and now it is time to walk authentically in my life. I will speak my truth. When I see my life from the position of the witness, I have a vantage point to adopt acceptance. Resistance to what I feel only creates suppressed (stuffed) emotions. That only adds to my pain body. By accepting all feelings, not acting on them just accepting them, I become calm. Accepting myself completely leads to acceptance of others as they are.

Lovingly,
River

Mantra for Today

October 16, 2021

No matter how long an addiction has been practiced to sooth a need, where there is life, there is hope for liberation. Being addicted is like being a slave to a demanding master. Financial resources and time and activities and mental focus are all directed towards the demands of the master. Just to know liberation is possible is the key to unlock the cell. The first step is willingness, then helpers rush in to assist in the mission. Today I will be in the possibility. Life has challenges. My mission statement is to practice acceptance, courage and wisdom. To have the courage to have the difficult conversation speaking my truth, asking for change. And if change isn't possible, accepting what is. And harvesting wisdom by noticing my reactions when things don't go my way. Today I cultivate self-acceptance while at the same time change.

Lovingly,
River

Mantra for Today

October 17, 2021

Being in an intimate relationship means embarking on a journey back to that first relationship between mother and child. When we are not aware that we have latent unmet dependency needs, we attack and try to control our partner because we have been so disappointed and frustrated in that primary relationship. When we are aware, we can consciously see what expectations we are putting on our partner to make us feel secure. Ironically when our partner is coerced to meet our needs they withdraw security. Today I will attempt to feel secure by nurturing kindness and forgiveness within myself and to my partner.

Lovingly,
River

Mantra for Today

October 18, 2021

Life has taught me to hold loosely to my plans for my day. Structure is great but when a friend in need makes a request, which will have a ripple effect on the days plans, I notice a tightening, this could turn into anxiety and resentment. Today I let go of what I think I must do, and let flow take me confidently in new directions. As I realize how much frustration I have been holding in my body, I become aware of my need to shift my priorities. Doing the same thing and expecting different results has unveiled an error in my approach. Today I will turn my attention inward, I will notice my feelings and practice self-compassion. Just giving feelings my attention is doing something different.

Lovingly,
River

Mantra for Today

October 19, 2021

I release in places where I previously held. I release resentments, I release jealousy, I release insecurity, I release fear. Today I accept myself even the negative qualities. I see clearly and make space. Today I will live as though this were my last day. Would I waste a minute of it. The purpose of my life is to live it as awake to reality as is possible. Realizing that as a divine being in human form I will bear all. I will have struggles the trick is to see I create them, and I can navigate them. I will have great joy; the trick is not to sabotage the experience with doubts and fears. Today I will practice being awake to reality and choose.

Lovingly,
River

Mantra for Today

October 20, 2021

When pure health is invaded by a cold or a flu, it's like our healthy energetic happy engaged self is locked away. Aches, loud hacking and coughing take up our otherwise peaceful space and we aren't inclined to socialize, nor is it good for anyone that we do. Today, I will lovingly retreat to the sick room and listen to my body. I must trust in a return to health. Challenges come from within and from others. I can only take responsibility for my part. Today I choose how I participate based on my word, my values, and my skills. When I'm clear about what I want most, I can see clearer when to be silent when invited to spar, when to speak when my commitment must be audible. And once I've spoken, silence speaks for me.

Lovingly,
River

Mantra for Today

October 21, 2021

All life is temporary, when somebody we care about leave their body it comes as a shock, we aren't ready for this. The grief comes in waves, there are moments of understanding and then comes the disbelief and shock again. There's nothing anyone can do but to go through it. There is such a thing as good grief, feeling your feelings embracing other people around you and cherishing this amazing temporary experience of life. The one who has passed is now on the Spirit Trail still with us in spirit form. The best we can do is honor them by grieving well. Today I will allow myself to both grieve a loss and celebrate the experience of life. Today, I will live in a good way.

Lovingly,
River

Mantra for Today

October 22, 2021

Relationships are built on trust; Trust is built when agreements are kept. Sometimes situations prevent the possibility of keeping agreements. New agreements allow trust to remain the firm foundation. Today I will keep my word and when that cannot be, I will renegotiate agreements, no drama, just good communication. There are situations that are out of my control. Wishing things were different than they are is futile and brings frustration. Today, I will practice self-care remain balanced by taking care of my body, mind, and soul. This may not change uncomfortable circumstances, but it supports me in living with them. People judge when fear takes hold of them. Seeing difference feels like a threat. Bigotry breeds violence. Being a target of violent attack can shake the inner foundation of security. In the face of judgment attitude trumps circumstance. Today I will see judgment as an opportunity to strengthen my relationship with myself.

Lovingly,
River

Mantra for Today

October 23, 2021

Where there is life, there is hope. Each day is an opportunity to expand into a fuller freer existence. Putting down the causes of suffering; the ideas and stories about self and other which are limiting, the substances that numb, the language that defends, the behaviors that are reactive. Today, this new day, I choose a new direction, and confront patterns and beliefs that have me stuck. It is sobering to realize that no one external to myself is able to make it all okay. Becoming a full-grown adult means replacing magical thinking that mom or dad or boyfriend/husband/girlfriend or wife is responsible to take care of my every need. The good news is the one I can count on never leaves my side and is always available, my higher self. Today I will build a healthy loving relationship with myself.

Lovingly,
River

Mantra for Today

October 24, 2021

Overcoming childhood trauma can feel worse before it gets better. The questions: "What's the point? Why am I here? Does my life matter? Bring sadness and loneliness. This is a time to trust. To be in the present moment with the sadness and focus on something simple and beautiful, like a flower or the many shades of color. Today I will care for myself by making this moment my safe place where I belong. When a younger part of myself felt unwanted or unworthy my best thinking reached for something to sooth the pain. Now is different, I know my value, yet, that part, that is outdated, still reaches. Today I will bring myself to current reality by listening to my child self and assure that part that old solutions don't serve anymore. I am willing to heal all of me, I choose a clean clear existence now.

Lovingly,
River

Mantra for Today

October 25, 2021

When a child experiences a trauma or begins using drugs or alcohol, their mental maturity becomes stuck at that specific stage of development, especially related to the trauma that made picking up and using seem like the answer. As a fully grown adult I am aware of my child brain, and childlike reaction. Today when child brain reacts, I pause and explore where this began. The goal is to integrate the emotional experience and bring my development up to date. My natural state of being is present, content, in joy and feeling affirmed. Worrisome thoughts bid for my attention taking me into a space quite unnatural. Today I will bring myself into the present moment attending to the here and now; now is always the time to focus on.

Lovingly,
River

Mantra for Today

October 26, 2021

I am accountable to ensure that I participate in relationships that support the highest good for all involved. When I allow negativity and blame to be expressed through me I create negativity in my relationship. When things seem to be falling apart I am in a prime position to take stock. Maybe a fresh start is called for, maybe a return to the terms of agreement in a relationship or maybe a clean break. Whatever is naturally called for I must first take full accountability for my part. Today I practice self-compassion and correct and continue. When I resist addressing something, I know I'm getting close to a breakthrough. Resistance feels like knots in my being; there is a repulsion and an urge to put the onus on something outside of me. When I address whatever I resist with a calm clear and conscious mindset I am empowered to transform a trauma into a new confidence within me. Today I will edge closer to that which I tend to resist.

Lovingly,
River

Mantra for Today

October 27, 2021

My life is a temporary experience. While here I must learn many fundamental truths. I must navigate emotions and weed out certain thoughts in order to live life as Mary Oliver would say: as, "a bride married to amazement". As for shame and guilt; I would ask to guilt, did I do something wrong? If yes, inspect it and correct it. If shame is felt it points to erroneous thinking and childhood conditioning, the practice of self-love and self-forgiveness is key. Shame has nothing to offer. Guilt is a sign correction is needed. It doesn't matter what people think of me, it doesn't matter that I still have a few qualities, such as self-confidence, in my "work in process" pile. What matters is that love in me shines to serve another on the path we both travel. Today I focus on service, the confidence and approval may come.

Lovingly,
River

Mantra for Today

October 28, 2021

When I do something out of obligation in order to be a good person, I am deceiving myself and others. Generosity is a gift from the heart. When obligation is felt, there is an opportunity to explore shame based programming and see how resentment grows organically from service based on shame. Today I will practice being authentic. I will make my yes a true yes otherwise it is no. There is a time for service to others and a time for self-care. Going to the inner well and drawing from source the life affirming and sustaining energy. Today stillness and gratitude; these are alchemy that transmutes stagnant energy into forward flowing love fuel.

Lovingly,
River

Mantra for Today

October 29, 2021

As long as I'm breathing, I have work to do. The car driving 20 MPH in front of me, "making" me late, is The Buddha. This experience is the clearest most accessible revaluation of where I need to work on myself. The litany of labels I assign to the driver, are labels I need to let go within, the diagnosis and judgments that freely flow from my lips, are criticisms I run in my own self attack. Today, I release aggression within myself and forgive the folly and foibles of others. Impatience is my teacher. The past does not hold me imprisoned. I forgive myself for reacting in ways that were unconscious. I ask others to forgive me and move forward in new more conscious ways. As long as I breath, possibilities are abundant for me to live with purpose. Today I am aware of who my people are. The one's who see me here and now. The imaginary future will unfold in a one thing at a time occurrence. I am most effective when at peace.

Lovingly,
River

Mantra for Today

October 30, 2021

The best relationships, the kind that really function to bring true comfort and satisfaction, are based on mutual respect and self-accountability. If one person in the relationship is an untreated addict, or has unresolved mental health problems, the relationship becomes imbalanced and can only lead to struggle. If I am in that kind of relationship I need to redirect my outpouring of care giving towards myself. What message am I giving myself that puts me in that kind of dynamic? What do I believe I deserve? Everything is always fertile ground for my growth. Today I create boundaries that serve to create healthy mutually rewarding connections with others; this is a practice of self care.

Lovingly,
River

Mantra for Today

October 31, 2021

There is a natural flow that, when I surrender to, brings peace. I cannot control the wind, I cannot control the rain, I cannot control another person's behavior. When I witness without desire (for anything other than what is) I am calm. I am not attached to my preferred ideas. Today I live in the calm place in myself that accepts what I cannot change. The sky is bright with stars and there is calm. The only thing to do is clean up the aftermath. Life is like this; emotions run high, time fills the open meadow of the day strewn with deadlines. When morning comes and clear thinking is back, what remains is the memory. Today I will remember that even though, when in a crisis, it feels like I am doomed, it will pass. Hunker down, pull my soft creature selves close for protection, and wait out the storm.

Lovingly,
River

Mantra for Today

November 1, 2021

Human being evolve through interactions. When a relationship is new, there is a euphoric feeling of confidence in self and the other; everything is going to be okay. A few months later, that chemical high dissipates, and the real purpose begins. We are in each other's lives to work with our unresolved emotional wounds. Transparency, owning our stuff, and boundaries create a map to healing and growth. Today I balance myself by having compassion for the journey.

Feelings of annoyance or irritation and anger in a relationship is predictable; being self contained in those moments is rare. When thoughts and feelings are unleashed and projected at another the relationship is put into crisis. Today, I will acknowledge my thoughts and feelings and take care of myself bringing myself back to my center. When centered I can communicate change with a better outcome.

Lovingly,
River

Mantra for Today

November 2, 2021

I read somewhere that happiness is an inside job; and yet the actions, choices and words of an intimate partner really influence the shared emotional space. It seems truer that steadiness and perspective, when practiced, regardless of another's mental health or moods, is a more achievable goal. Today I choose to support my health by choosing what inspires me and brings me joy even when it is my unique experience. If I travel back in time long long ago, I see the women of society honored and revered for their contribution. I hear the council of women coaching the people, passing on their wisdom teachings. Somehow things took a turn and women became oppressed, subservient, silenced and seen as human vending machines. As a result, addiction, eating disorders, self-loathing replaced feminine purpose and place. Today I will listen carefully to the voice of the grandmothers. I will honor the gifts with gratitude of the women today and point her back to her innate wisdom.

Lovingly,
River

Mantra for Today

November 3, 2021

Yes, there are a lot of difficulties in life, there are emotional challenges; but when I hold my head up high when I put my shoulders back and I allow my spine to lengthen and greet people with an audible hello with eye contact; everything in my world gets just a little bit better. This posture give myself and others the message that I am an example of hope. Today I will raise the energy by standing tall.

Lovingly,
River

Mantra for Today

November 4, 2021

In a world heavily populated by humans I am called to evolve into an accountable, emotionally mature full grown adult. Even though the big people in my childhood did not portray balanced, grounded or safe representation of adulthood. I can choose to use their examples of what not to be. I am an artistic masterpiece in my own right. I will find the grownups to model my life by. I am on a healing hero's journey.

Lovingly,
River

Mantra for Today

November 5, 2021

When an idea or belief of what something means is held so tightly, there is no space for other possible explanations. By exploring various possibilities, or better yet, seeking the truth through direct inquiry life becomes easier. Today I question long held views and choose peace.

Lovingly,
River

Mantra for Today

November 6, 2021

Perfectionism is a form of mental anguish. Whether it's cleaning the shelf to the point of taking off the varnish, or eating so clean that a social gathering becomes a obsessive inquiry, or behavior and speech are rewound and analyzed to the point of distraction perfectionism is suffering. Today, I will allow "good enough", and get on with living. It's all just simple, good enough.

Lovingly,
River

Mantra for Today

November 7, 2021

When I can laugh, I know I've crossed over the worst of it all. All the fumbles and bumbles of ego lead behaviors, so vehemently protected and defended as I feel around in the darkness self-centered and self-serving, wondering why my life is in shambles all comes to the clearing when the lights go on; maybe it's not all about me and maybe it is all about me. These two truths sharing stage as I shift my course of right thinking, right acting. I choose to drop my defenses and take a suggestion.

Lovingly,
River

Mantra for Today

November 8, 2021

Resentments retard my relationships. Making enemies, in my mind, with beloved friend's or family's behavior gives me a false sense of superiority assigning myself as their judge. Quietly held seething feelings while at the same time going through the motions of the relationship is toxic. We are all works in progress; speaking my experience with self-accountability invites change and growth. Today I speak my truth and let it go, this is freedom.

Lovingly,
River

Mantra for Today

November 8, 2021

I create the life I want to live by having the courage to turn and face the stories I tell myself about myself, others and about what's possible. It takes courage to realize the mind's version of reality very well may only be a partial reality. By living based on half-truths, there is a high risk of error. If actions are based on false pretense, well it can be catastrophic! Today I get real. The new T. V Series, Tidying Up, with Marie Kondo inspires living without clutter. The series is based on physical space but imagine opening the mental closet and piling all beliefs that no longer serve on the kitchen table! One by one asking does this belief bring me joy? If no, thank it for being part of your story and toss into the "let go" basket. Today I uncluttered my mind from joy robbing thoughts.

Lovingly,
River

Mantra for Today

November 9, 2021

Every cell in my being is listening. There is a vibrational frequency in every living being. The trees communicate with each other through a certain frequency. So, it is with my body. I raise the frequency through conscious truth talk. Negative self-talk are old tapes recorded based on fear. If there is no imminent danger right now, I choose to see life and myself as unfolding perfectly, in harmony with the divine vibration of good to very good, all good. I'm as sick as my secrets. Truth is known in the body, locked in with a combination of traumatic incidents. Speaking my truth opens my heart, my joy, my treasure chest of gifts. Truth is the key to freedom. Today, I take risks in telling my truth, fear has no place in my freedom.

Lovingly,
River

Mantra for Today

November 10, 2021

Relationships offer constant opportunities to become the one we are capable of being. Relationship is the beloved container to bring what needs healing from the traumas of childhood. The trick is to hold space for the others healing while not becoming enmeshed. Today, I practice awareness regarding my triggers from childhood, I am accountable not to project my childhood wounds onto another. I identify what is mine and what is not mine. Harmony. Today a word from The Handbook To Higher Consciousness: "I feel, with love and compassion, the problems of others without getting caught up in the predicaments that are theirs for their growth". Ken Keyes. Each individual is on their own path. When I try to impose my solutions on another person's problems there may be resistance. Our problems are sign posts, they point us to what needs addressing in our lives. The first step is willingness.

Lovingly,
River

Mantra for Today

November 10, 2021

My interaction today is to take back my power. Areas where I feel weak; whether it is in my personal self-management or response while with others, I will ground myself in the truth of my existence. I belong, I am worthy. My power is in knowing this and from this basic knowing I stand in love.

Lovingly,
River

Mantra for Today

November 11, 2021

I have been graced with a body that has forgiven me, that has carried me and has endured and survived so much. Today I will be gracious in return to this beautiful body by listening to what it needs most. I forgive myself for overriding its requests for compassion and kindness. Today I will still my mind and be present to my body's highest good. I honor this life and renew my commitment to choosing to attend to what is called for now. This is not a sacrifice this is an offering.

Lovingly,
River

Mantra for Today

November 12, 2021

My life is a dynamic story. What is happening right now, is changing as I speak. Today, I will have a conversation with my future me. I will encourage my current self with visions of my future self while at the same time honoring who I am now. Future self, you've lived a good life, you got through some extraordinary times, you've had losses and gains, way to keep growing! Some days the body hurts, sleep is interrupted, and I struggle to accept this reality. These are days to lower my expectations and to be gentle with myself. In every life experience there are gifts and opportunities. By dropping into what is I gentle my experience. This too shall pass. I am blessed with eyes to see! What comes into focus depends on what I look at. I have a good brain, what I concentrate on becomes pivotal. Choosing what I place my attention on is choosing my experience. Am I going to dwell on the dust or look up and see the vast wonder? Am I going to see the puddle on the road or the ocean? Will I give central stage to the faults of another or their vast goodness? It's all a choice.

Lovingly,
River

Mantra for Today

November 13, 2021

"When you are at peace with yourself, anyplace is home". My kuliana, is to be a friend to myself, caring for my needs and making my dreams come true. As I learn to speak kindly, I transform the words from criticism to encouragement. Slowly I become native to my life and see, it is me that creates happiness and not external circumstances. The greatest prayer is how I live my life. I play many parts on the stage of life, as an adult service is one of them, however, if I don't have self-care as a priority, and if I put my own needs for ritual soul serving nature walks on the back burner, I fool myself into thinking serving others is the highest value. Balancing my service to myself by sculpting out time for exercise that soothes my soul and supports my body with service to others raises my effectiveness and presence to a higher quality of sacred service.

Lovingly,
River

Mantra for Today

November 14, 2021

Last day of the year! Imaging all the amazing experiences of the year well lived, I become clear that who I am at my core is not going to change. I let go of constant assessment, I let go of criticism and I allow freedom. Letting go is inviting space. Today I still my mind and allow the clarity of true knowing to inform me. Life is precious and I am life.

Lovingly,
River

Mantra for Today

November 15, 2021

New beginnings offer fresh inspiration to set the sights in my chosen direction. Yesterday is gone, I've let go of some of the attachments, today I continue to wiggle out of habits that aren't helpful. My helpers are both spiritual and human. The direction of self -are requires I drop any harsh evaluation and adopt loving empathy. It all begins with clearing the mind of harmful thoughts and surrendering to the unknown path, the un-storied song, that awaits.

Lovingly,
River

Mantra for Today

November 16, 2021

Getting crystal clear on what matters to me helps me participate in ways that invites that in. Treating the people that matter to me with appreciation, patience and words of love draws them closer with unshielded authenticity. Owning my emotional reactions, I soften my words. The words I use are friendly and uplifting not judging or damaging. If I become triggered and know I am going to burst with sharp tongued attack, I excuse myself. That is my small self-needing a time out. I promise to return the same day I reconnect and redirect us back on track.

The people in my life are fellow classmates in this earth school. Some, as the poem goes, are in my life for a reason. We come together for a brief, yet deeply impacting, time. When relationships end, I consider my contribution to all aspects of it, and humbly bow in gratitude for the journey and its end. I honor myself by harvesting wisdom and letting go with grace.

Lovingly,
River

Mantra for Today

November 17, 2021

"Guilding the leading edge of a new day, with the purity of its un-storied song". Anything is possible in this un-storied day, I have little control but how I set forth my energy, choosing to say yes to something consciously is saying no to something else. What am I saying yes to? That is the question. Routines support balance. Holiday times encourage indulgence. As I weigh the cost and benefits, I realize maintaining my balance feels best. Enjoying the special treats available during the holiday while at the same time honoring my need for balance results in maximum enjoyment with no regrets. I choose consciously to enjoy an 80/20 approach. 80% routine and 20% free fall. I am in balance.

Lovingly,
River

Mantra for Today

November 18, 2021

We all need empathy and validation. When a relationship goes off the rails, Non- Violent Communication is called for. This means listening with compassion and understanding. When needs are unmet, people become imbalanced. Asking, "what do you need, how can I give that to you, while still having my own needs met? Begins the conversation towards getting back on track.

Relationships that address conflicts with "right or wrong" score sheets result in hurt and disconnection. Seeing the other with criticism and intolerance and blame results in disharmony, yet, harmony is the goal. When the relationship I have with myself is one of self -acceptance and self-empathy, I participate with others in ways that bring a better outcome. I can give the love I give myself.

Lovingly,
River

Mantra for Today

November 19, 2021

When I think of all the ways I use being nice in order to avoid conflict, I see how I become weaker inside. Today I will deliver my truth with transparency, I am not responsible for other people's reaction. When I speak my truth, others also have opportunity to interact authentically. When I reflect on my interactions with others, I see my imperfections. I am a work in process; with self-compassion and self-forgiveness, I am humbly accountable. I make amends and move forward. I am perfectly imperfect.

Lovingly,
River

Mantra for Today

November 20, 2021

Everyone wants to be loved unconditionally. When I am in a difficult situation with another person, I feel compassion and see they are suffering. I don't get caught up in their problem, I hold space and give space without getting entangled emotionally. I offer my love by staying centered and at peace. Breathing in I am filled, breathing out I let go. I forgive myself for wanting to solve another's suffering, that is there for their growth. If they attack me, out of unconsciousness, I take space and care for myself with unconditional love.

Lovingly,
River

Mantra for Today

November 21, 2021

Acceptance and Change. I accept who I am. I see myself from the neutral place of the Observer, (without judgment). I see how I have been shaped by my experiences, the good, the bad and the ugly. As I notice, I see the qualities in myself that are precious. I also realize certain ways of being that create negative results in my life and relationships. Through acceptance of myself, warts and all, and self-acknowledgment of my gifts. I can begin to change my habits and thoughts more in alignment with my higher good. I accept myself and also choose to change. Be a yes person to life today. Let the supply of good flow towards you. Resist nothing, allow even the struggle to teach you what you need to learn so that you can be as free as you are meant to be.

Lovingly,
River

Mantra for Today

November 22, 2021

When I take a sober look at my thinking followed by behavior, it's like a light shines brightly on self-created suffering. I suddenly see the error and the solution. The thread is easily followed from the effect to the cause. I can change my thinking error and walk differently. I forgive myself. Criticism doesn't inspire, punishment doesn't correct. Today I commit to words and responses, towards myself and others, that come from a place of compassion and love. I turn critic into coach.

Lovingly,
River

Mantra for Today

November 23, 2021

I am the writer, director, and narrator, of my own movie titled: My Life. Sharing the stage are the judge, the critic, the inner child, the shamer, the controller, the helper, etc. etc. The important thing to remember is, none of them are the lead. By consciously attending to their scripts, I create my masterpiece theater. Today's episode is, A Life Lived With Ease.

I belong to the church of what wants to happen. Letting go of a need to control and instead dropping into what IS allows me to be spacious. Lowering expectations is a practice of acceptance. Even though I may have preferences different than what is presently happening; shifting towards what IS brings contentment.

Lovingly,
River

Mantra for Today

November 24, 2021

I acknowledge that when my mind offers me fearful thoughts, it is not necessarily true. When I push past fear, I build confidence. I am the master of my mind, not the other way around.

I release the need to control people and situations. There is a freedom felt when I see everything, that is out of my control, as perfect. I exchange control for ease and grace. Grace brings radical acceptance and letting go of struggle for control brings ease. Life never seizes to offer opportunities to grow. When I step out of my "already know" or "I'm right" stance, and step into curiosity and especially remember my intentions for the relationship, I loosen up relax and listen with an open mind and open heart. I may not always agree, I may choose to act based on different values than another, yet still respectfully remain in unconditional love.

Lovingly,
River

Mantra for Today

November 25, 2021

Today is a day of Thanksgiving. Strange times for most of us where we would be spending time with family and beloved friends. The COVID restrictions may mean that is not in the cards this year. Is this fortunate or unfortunate? We don't know. It is easy to decide where one event or circumstance is preferred and another destained. From a position of not knowing, there is an opening for a broader possibility to occur. Refrain from judging and see what surprises await in every situation. Whether a thing is good or bad is really only a manufactured idea. Who would you be without a preferred outcome today? Today I will practice openness to what wants to happen and wait and see if there may be blessings in disguise.

Lovingly,
River

Mantra for Today

November 26, 2021

My spirit is lifted up when I remember the generosity of my ancestors who have carved the path before me, behind me. Today I give generously to others as a ceremony signifying the flow of everything. Being fearful in scarcity mentality cinches off the circulation of abundance. I trust in giving and receiving. Today I acknowledge I am blessed. The people in my life are mirrors for me. When the reflection is offered with kindness and genuine support, I can manage easy acceptance and change. When it is offered through anger and criticism, I see more a projection of their unresolved emotional charges. It is less helpful in the form of criticism. Today I practice discernment. I am a worthy being of loving kindness. I will make every word a word of love.

Lovingly,
River

Mantra for Today

November 27, 2021

I will see my life and relationships through beginners mind. That means I don't have expectations nor already know what it will be like. I return again and again to my source of love, and from this safe place I can freely be in new ways. I love my life! I support myself and improve my experiences when I choose affirming words to define myself and others. Life says "yes" to whatever word I use. If I say, my family loves and supports me, life says, yes! If I say, I'm not valuable to them, life says, yes! There are a multitude of possible ways of seeing any situation. Today I focus on the view and use words that expand my heart and open my mind to more possibilities.

Lovingly,
River

Mantra for Today

November 28, 2021

Today I will turn my words and thoughts to express gratitude. Where there is disappointment, I will see beneath the blessings in disguise. Where there is complaint, I will see the reality of perfection in everything. Where discontentment, I will choose present moment acceptance. All are expressions of gratitude. Today I will give Thanks. My life is evidence of a miracle. The very reality of my existence is awe inspiring. It is up to me how I live this life. By leaving the past and being in the present I make moment to moment adjustments which support possibilities in my future. Today I will practice presence., starting with conscious breath. I love my life.

Lovingly,
River

Mantra for Today

November 29, 2021

I notice when I try to control things I become tightly wound up inside. I will practice shifting demands into preferences and allow more possibilities. "I prefer..." Instead of, "I demand, require, expect and if I don't get it that way I will have a melt-down". I transform my experience when I shift demands into preferences and trust that what happens will be in the highest good for all involved. Everyone wants to be loved unconditionally. When I am in a difficult situation with another person, I feel compassion and see they are suffering. I don't get caught up in their problem, I hold space and give space without getting entangled emotionally. I offer my love by staying centered and at peace. Breathing in I am filled, breathing out I let go. I forgive myself for wanting to solve another's suffering, that is there for their growth. If they attack me, out of unconsciousness, I take space and care for myself with unconditional love.

Lovingly,
River

Mantra for Today

November 30, 2021

I am learning to be aware of when I am triggered. I realize that my reaction, whether it be anger, fear or sadness, is pointing to the fact that an emotion from long ago is still alive in me. The situation that is triggering me today is an opportunity to discharge that long held fear, anger, or sadness which settled into my system at a time when I couldn't understand things as well as I do now. The current situation is an opportunity to apply new perspectives which inspire me rather than cause reactions. This discharges the long held emotion, and I am less burdened, more liberated.

Lovingly,
River

Mantra for Today

December 1, 2021

Words are powerful. I choose words carefully, especially words that describe who I am. My body, mind and soul are supported and respond positively to loving and encouraging words. As I become more conscious I re-language my thoughts and speech to direct my life in affirming ways. My system responds to the words I use.

Lovingly,
River

Mantra for Today

December 2, 2021

I am a constantly changing being. Each of my life's experiences, especially the painful ones, have helped me grow. I forgive myself and others, thereby letting go of the pain and harvest the lessons. Sort the valuable from the worthless. As I pause to notice my maturing, I acknowledge possibilities. With willingness, vs willfulness I am open.

Lovingly,
River

Mantra for Today

December 2, 2021

As I reflect on my actions of the past, I see what in particular brings me suffering. When my mind offers me an idea, that something or someone is a threat to me, and I react defensively I create drama. Drama creates problems and problems are exhausting. I am aware that these patterns are all I know, they are automatic. I have not accepted people's suggestions to do things differently because I am uncomfortable with the unknown (uncertain) future. Today I wise up. I choose to surrender my mind's ideas and am willing to do something different and see what wants to happen.

Lovingly,
River

Mantra for Today

December 3, 2021

I freely accept the generosity of the universe. Gifts are signals that I am loved. Words of kindness and compliments are messages from others of their experience of my divinity. I openly receive all the good that flows towards me, there is abundance. I notice my scarcity mentality when I act as though I don't deserve or can't afford to accept the loving gestures and generosity of others. I open myself to expand where I am constricted.

Lovingly,
River

Mantra for Today

December 4, 2021

The earth we live on, is our school. It is not surprising that I feel constantly offered opportunity to learn. Like any successful student, when I stop complaining, stop comparing myself to others, stop blaming my teachers, I mature, I learn, I grow, and it all becomes easier. To be an astute student in life is to accept that at times it is hard, but not impossible. Eventually I "get it". Understanding resources us to be on solid ground in the face of struggles.

Lovingly,
River

Mantra for Today

December 5, 2021

Mistakes are expected, inspected, accepted, and corrected. My motto is "correct and continue". I learned this from NASA. When their rockets are off course they simply, correct and continue. There is no need to create an identity for myself based on my mistakes, I learn and forgive myself, from forgiveness, I continue with a clean slate. The past offers one essential gift, experience, learn from it, and let it go.

Lovingly,
River

Mantra for Today

December 6, 2021

Byran Katie is a world-renowned speaker and author of, The Work. Her methods support inquiring thoughts. My mind is at times like an annoying roommate; nitpicking, critical and constantly judging. Today I will recognize that my mind and I are not one, today I will challenge my mind by asking, Is it true? How am I when I believe this to be true? Who would I be if I did not believe this to be true? What else is true? By inquiring, I offer myself support and compassion.

Lovingly,
River

Mantra for Today

December 7, 2021

Acceptance and commitment therapy (ACT) supports clients in learning to accept what is. This does not mean we are happy with what is, but as we learn to accept rather than resist we develop a better relationship with reality. From a clear position of seeing, we can choose. When we are clear about what we want to create, our goals based on our values, we begin the process of change. No plant grows where first there was no seed. In me are seeds of peace and seeds of problems, which ever I water with produce either a healthy plant or weeds. As I train my mind, I tend the garden of my dreams. Weeding out thoughts that choke out my joy.

Lovingly,
River

Mantra for Today

December 8, 2021

When situations become tense with another person, I practice breathing in to the count of 7, hold it, and breath out to the count of 8. I do this 3 times. I imagine my mind becoming like a still pond. Then I respond rather than react. It does me no good to become twisted in my mind, turning the story over and over. I do what I can, and accept what I have no control over, that is other people. I choose to be peace.

Lovingly,
River

Mantra for Today

December 9, 2021

I am the author and director of my own movie; today I will choose the thoughts and actions that support my vision of a day lived well. At the end of the day, I will ask myself: did I serve myself and others? Was I present spiritually in loving kindness? Did I forgive myself and others for big and little foibles? Each day I am born to create.

Lovingly,
River

Mantra for Today

December 10, 2021

One needs to be in a place of readiness in order to receive the goodness offered. The greatest intentions to help another person may be fruitless efforts if the one in need has obstacles in the way. It may be constructs of not deserving, suspicions of motive, the egos refusal to appear needy, or fear that there's a catch. Whatever the obstruction, the timing of the offer to ease the load may be off. The practice of non attachment offers ease around giving and receiving. I trust everything happens for our growth into higher consciousness, including the struggles. I will not take it personal.

Lovingly,
River

Mantra for Today

December 11, 2021

It is easy to place responsibility on others when you are triggered. In the past, someone acted in ways that left you feeling abandoned. You were less resourced to understand all the dynamics of the situation so made it mean there was something wrong with you personally. It is possible to cloud the present with the past and collapse a new person in your life with the one you believe harmed you. Be accountable for the experience dear one, it is unfair to place a template of the past onto someone in your life who may very well be trying to help you. Everything is an opportunity for healing. Remind yourself of your resilience and wisdom gained from life's challenges. Everything is conspiring for your highest good.

Lovingly,
River

Mantra for Today

December 12, 2021

This one life you are living is your work in progress. You are an individual in a relationship with everything. You do not exist alone, like everything else you are part of a whole. Develop empathy for your fellow beings; they too are on a journey of feelings, decisions, faced with their delusions of reality. Each of us are interdependent and at the same time responsible for our own evolution. To evolve is to grow out of small mind, to face our self pity and love ourselves into reality. We are worthy, we belong. May all beings be free.

Lovingly,
River

Mantra for Today

December 13, 2021

Acceptance and Commitment therapy is an approach that focuses on a non judgemental "seeing" of aspects or behaviors of ours that are not helpful. Shame does not inspire growth, there is no useful quality in harsh self assessment. Change comes gradually as we make choices to move in new ways. Ways that do not drop us back into unconscious habits. Today is a new day. Asking yourself, "what do you need sweetheart", is a loving approach in taking yourself by the hand and guiding your life with new thoughts and actions that lead to what you want and need more than the old patterns offered.

Lovingly,
River

Mantra for Today

December 14, 2021

We are born uniquely who we are. We come into this life wired for connection, yet when we don't find that bonding with our families, we feel wrong somehow. It is important to take an expanded view of what all is contributing to this alienation. Our parents may not be equipped to provide the warmth and attention we need. This doesn't diminish our worthiness for loving support. There is a collective programming based on lack that when basic needs are all that is provided, and there is no space for addressing spiritual needs; this programming focuses on functioning only, not on celebrating that unique being that you are. It is time to stop taking it personally and claim your own life. Begin to forgive parents and find your own path of contentment. We don't truly grow up until we fire our parents from the role of defining us.

Lovingly,
River

Mantra for Today

December 15, 2021

To be a fully evolved being, we must shed our obsession with ourselves. Self-insight and understanding are a valuable process for growth, and, simultaneously awareness of our fellow humans is evidence of evolution. Consideration for self and other, creates a world of peace and compassion. Too much "self, me, mine" leads to narcissistic neediness which misses the bigger picture, cohabitation. Today I will focus on both self-growth and understanding as well as service to my brothers and sisters (both human and animal), on planet earth. I am responsible for the love in my world. Lovingly, River

Lovingly,
River

Mantra for Today

December 16, 2021

When one embraces the reality of impermanence, changes don't have to be frightening. It is the stories we tell ourselves and the meaning we make that make a thing acceptable or catastrophic. Like the song by the Byrds, Turn! Turn! Turn! To every thing there is a season. Today I flow comfortably with change and refrain from thought generating fears. It is all very natural.

Lovingly,
River

Mantra for Today

December 17, 2021

Self love is the foundation of a good life. Past hurts confuse us, our child self believes we somehow attracted those hurts by doing something wrong. Trust wains and the relationship with self suffers. We carry on an inner dialogue of blame, negative evaluations; a defeating narrative runs like the sound track of a horror film. Today, begin to change. Drop the heavy bag of the past. Start developing trust in self by remaining in the present moment. Use affirming supportive language. Treat yourself like you would a beloved child. Today I trust.

Lovingly,
River

Mantra for Today

December 18, 2021

Self-Emptying

Letting Go Is Liberation

In talking about letting go, we are really talking about liberation. It's a type of liberation theology for a Global North country, if you will. Here are the proper questions: What is it we need to be liberated from, and what is it we need to be liberated for? And who is the liberator?

I think we need at least six kinds of liberation:

1. Inner liberation from ourselves (letting go of the centrality of the small self)
2. Cultural liberation from our biases (which involves letting go of the "commodity" culture and moving into the "personal" culture) [1]
3. Dogmatic liberation from our certitudes (letting go of the false self and discovering the True Self)
4. Personal liberation from the "system" (letting go of dualistic judging and opening to nondual thinking)
5. Spiritual liberation *for* the Divine (some form of letting go happens between each stage of spiritual growth)
6. Liberation *for* infinite mystery (the mystery that what looks like falling is in fact rising), which is really liberation for love.

As you have often heard me say, *if you do not transform your pain, you will most assuredly transmit it.* Healthy religion on the practical level tells us what to do with our pain—because we will have pain. We can't avoid it; it's part of life. If we're not trained in letting go of it, transforming it, turning crucifixion into resurrection, so to speak, we'll hand it off to our family, to our children, to our neighborhood, to our nation.

The art of letting go is really the art of survival. We have to let go so that as we age, we can be happy. Yes, we've been hurt. Yes, we've been talked about and betrayed by friends. Yes, our lives didn't work out the way we thought they would. Letting go helps us fall into a deeper and broader level at which we can always say "Yes." We can always say, "It's okay, it's all right." We know what lasts. We know who we are. And we know we do not want to pass our pain on to our children or the next generation. We want to somehow pass on life.

This means that the real life has started now. It's Heaven all the way to Heaven and it's Hell all the way to Hell. We are in Heaven now by falling, by letting go, and by trusting and surrendering to this deeper, broader, and better reality that is already available to us. We're in Hell now by wrapping ourselves around our hurts, by over-identifying with and attaching ourselves to our fears, so much so that they become our very identity. Any chosen state of victimhood is an utter dead end. Once you make that your narrative, it never stops gathering evidence about how you have been wronged by life, by others, and even by God.

Maybe this is why scholars have said two-thirds of the teaching of Jesus is, in one form or another, about forgiveness. Forgiveness is simply the religious word for letting go. Eventually, it feels like forgiving Reality Itself for being what it is.

Lovingly,
River

Mantra for Today

December 19, 2021

Sometimes in love relationships there are underlying childhood issues interfering with intimacy. Depending on how each person in the relationship was mothered there is either vulnerability and a free expressions of needs and feelings or there is inability and a protective armor blocking this deep connection. It can be very confusing to be in this type of dynamic. There are lessons in everything; and one of the lessons in this type of dynamic is to learn not to take things personally. We've all shied away from the term codependency, yet codependency is a result when interacting in a unclear energy field with another person. We want to feel safe and secure so we start to over identify with our partner's feelings and needs. Remember always that everything is grace, everything is on our path for our growth. Today remember, don't take anything personally and do your best. Turn within and find security there. This is the best bet to move in life on a solid foundation.

Lovingly,
River

Mantra for Today

December 20, 2021

"Should I stay or should I go now"? When I am of 2 minds, I create instability and mental chaos. Training my mind to be present in each moment guides me to participate with commitment and willingness. If I show up fully, I contribute in ways that create security and self-confidence. Today, no matter how hard, I choose to stay on course.

There is a surface identity that is my outer appearance. If I place my measurement of worth on other's evaluation of this small aspect of me, I become a slave to an unstable variable of opinions. My true nature, the core of me, is where my beauty only grows greater. Today I begin disidentifying with the shallow shell of appearance, and deeply express my true self through my values and loving kindness. I have worth beyond all appearance. Lovingly River

Lovingly,
River

Mantra for Today

December 21, 2021

Forgiveness is freedom. The anger that lives just beneath the surface is like a toxin saturating every cell. This chemical reaction binds so tightly and weaves into a rope. When we recognize that holding onto resentments is like being tied to a post, then we can untie the rope that binds us, forgive and move on. It is for the sake of freedom that we forgive. Living bound to another through hurt and anger is no different that being handcuffed to them. Today I remind myself, I am angry due to unmet needs, I release others from responsibility to meet my needs and I address my needs in creative new ways.

Lovingly,
River

Mantra for Today

December 22, 2021

Sweetness attracts where sour averts. Finding fault in another and expressing their failings is an unlikely way to invoke cooperation. Being right and angrily making your point, will unlikely result in full agreement and accommodation. Change is not easy dear one, but full accountability for your behavior, humbly admitting where you contributed to the conflict positions you in a masterful place of leadership. Today, i will address my attitude and take one step towards a more equanimity in my relationships.

Lovingly,
River

Mantra for Today

December 23, 2021

The human experience is complicated. We are impressionable by experiences when we are too young to fully understand. These impressions stay with us as beliefs. Then as we interface with the world of people, changes, and losses we may feel ill equipped to deal with it all. Each of us has characteristics of that described in the DSM (manual of mental diagnosis) at any given snap shot moment of distress. The key is to be compassionate and forgiving. Today I will be my own best friend; lovingly validating my experience with, "it makes sense that you feel this way right now, let's make the next moment better". Focusing on the wisdom harvested from the pain I, am resourced.

Lovingly,
River

Mantra for Today

December 24, 2021

There are masterful ways to live, and there are un-skillful ways to live. It is never too late to practice the former. What does a master look like? One who sees the truth as opposed to mind made up versions of reality. How do I see truth? Stick to the facts, stick to what is evident, stay here and now. What is un-skillful? Doubting one's worth, worrying, and placing your power in the hands of others. Today, I will ask for what I need and accept. I will breath slowly and support my here and now reality.

Lovingly,
River

Mantra for Today

December 25, 2021

Christmas can be a day of festivities and cheer as people gather to fellowship lovingly infused with traditional flare, or it can be a time of loss, loneliness and the vacancy of what feels "should be". It is an opportunity as we globally address a pandemic to lift our sights to a higher vision than our own personal preferences. Perspective is everything. Magical thinking can really play tricks on the mind, even causing depression. Lift your spirits today no matter what your unique reality, regardless of the new and different Christmas you are having and tap into that private space within yourself, that place of bliss that awaits your attention. Let go of expectations and be with what is in complete acceptance. Maui Blissness to you dear one. I love you.

Lovingly,
River

Mantra for Today

December 26, 2021

The main task towards adulthood is to being self aware. Life's bumps and bruises, insults and injury can leave a person reactive. Blaming others for how we feel only keeps us stuck. At times, it is easy to feel victimized when misunderstood we react, rebuke, defend and attack back. Non of these reactions feel like choices but they are. On some level the mind is committed to a certain view. Thoughts lead to feeling which lead to actions and reactions. This is the basic tenet of Cognitive Behavioral Therapy, CBT. Once the emotions settle down, take the time to expand the thought process and see what else is true. Sometimes getting space from what is stimulating the thoughts is helpful. Meditation and prayer can take you to higher ground where a calmer mind offers new insights. Be aware beloved one, life is not trying to harm you.

Lovingly,
River

Mantra for Today

December 27, 2021

Each of us has our gifts to contribute on the stage of relationship. When those offerings are seen as valuable by one another and they complement each other a harmonious symphony ensues. But when we want a relationship so badly, we may avert our eyes and ignore obvious signs that together of stage we will be a romantic heart break. Try as we might to force compatibility, the obvious mismatch leaves us sad and lonely. You are loved dear one and worthy of a perfect fit. Tolerate the loneliness and trust. Love of life itself will fill the space held for the one.

Lovingly,
River

Mantra for Today

December 28, 2021

It is our sole responsibility to create what we envision for ourselves and our lives. The ones around us are not the holders of the key to our healing, fixing, or transformations. To come face to face with reality and take a humble and honest look at our behavior, and to admit how our participation has resulted in a high vibration connection or a low vibration depression is to take the steering wheel and choose our course. Yes we need the help of others, this is grace, but nothing can change without a personal commitment to be and do that which makes the difference. Today I hold myself in loving embrace and turn my face to the sun. Possibilities await my action.

Lovingly,
River

Mantra for Today

December 29, 2021

As the year comes to an end, I make peace with the year's end. Thankful for the journey. There were people who came, touched me, and left. People who stayed. There were ways I contributed, there was growth. Like a construct, I build on each experience; one lesson informs another lesson and wisdom builds and if I'm to remain another year, more lessons, more growth, more learning, more wisdom and more pain too. Today I begin the practice of becoming comfortable with loss. As long as I live loss and gain, death and birth are my experience.

Lovingly,
River

Mantra for Today

December 30, 2021

We are blessed when another generously holds space as the pieces are laid out, and the effort to see the puzzle picture is shared. You are not alone dear one. As you move majestically and calmly, you will eventually find it is all beautiful. The first step is the accept what is, the next step is to choose to remain tethered to your values. Make your choices based on what is most important to you. And celebrate true friends and trust shared wisdom.

Lovingly,
River

Mantra for Today

December 31, 2021

New Year's Eve is a good time to contemplate the very real experience of change. It has been a day publicly proclaimed as a poignant day of reflection. The new year has been ceremonially seen as a blank canvas on which to create the life that beckons you to live. Think, when have you been happiest? Think of when you have been the least happy. From this, contemplate how can I lead my life in the direction of my true purpose? You are the author of your own story; all the co stars and back drops have been fabulous for your growth; giving you power to discern what is right for you. Be gentle and gradual with your writing of the new scenes for your life in 2021. What needs to change? What stays? The direction of focus is inward, as you focus your light the external changes effortlessly. Happy New Year precious!

Lovingly,
River

These mantras have been inspired by my teachers, Katherine Woodward Taylor, Barbra Marx Hubbard, Mooji, Katie Byron, Louise Haye, Lesta Bertoia, who among the many wisdom keepers and visionaries offer new thought in the face of the global pandemic. When we can take the position of observer, we see that crisis proceeds transformation. Reflect on your own life, do you see how your challenging times led to growth and change? Belonging is one of our fundamental needs; if early in life we felt less than embraced and cherished, we developed certain cravings and attachments.

2021 has brought to the surface anxiety, fears and doubt in many of us. Social isolation through stay at home mandates, faces half hidden behind masks and restricted access to familiar services and community events. This has driven people into darkness and despair. In so many ways the pandemic has thwarted people's healthy routines; news feeds fill the space we dwell with the rising number of deaths and forecasts for a future of insecurity and loneliness.

The light carriers and wisdom teachers have used the online forum to reach out to people offering messages of hope for a new normal. These messages in juxtaposition of the doom of the media invite humanity to create intentions for the new year; to rise up out of 2020 harvesting the good from the pause in our robotic lives. We have been given space to address automatic toxic thoughts that run like a sound track in our minds. Thoughts and opinion about ourselves and others and the world in general gone unchecked. The new year nudges us towards an invitation to open ourselves to a new reality. New perspective which are born from stillness offer us a waking up from our sleep walking. It is time to relate to yourself and the world with a more empowered narrative of self love and acceptance. We contribute to the greater good of the collective by first giving ourselves the judgment free acceptance that we needed in childhood, then we can be open hearted to others and participate in a gentler way.

COVID 19 has given us an opportunity to appreciate nature, to value our freedom, to not take for granted the ease of which we once moved. There are blessings in disguise as we see clearly, we did not move with ease; we moved in a rat race driven by productivity and a vague sense of success, in order to feel secure.

The dark night is breathing deeply waking us up to a new day. 2021 has been a year of opportunity. Take a moment each day to consciously complete on unfinished conversations and long held hurts. Finish the past with a powerful note claiming your gift, the lesson learned.

From completion we are renewed.

It has been my hearts delight to hold these conversations with you. Each mantra was inspired by a direct relationship between me and you. We are not separate in our life's dynamic events of emotions and feelings. You are never alone! No matter if your personality is sensitive or your shell has hardened or you have withdrawn or you reach out and express, you are in a shared human experience and you matter!

You, my dear one, are divine in human form.

My intention in sharing with you is that you may be lifted up by these mantras and that you put your burden down.

In hearts fullest love!

Lovingly,
River

CPSIA information can be obtained
at www.ICGtesting.com
Printed in the USA
BVHW031622050621
608858BV00001B/1